Tana

He
Leadeth
Me

May the Lord continue to bless & use you for His glory!

Shirley's Soliloquies,
Volume V
2014

Lovingly,
Shirley Hudson
July 2015

by

Shirley Hudson

HE LEADETH ME
Copyright © 2014 by Shirley L. Hudson

All rights reserved. No part of this book may be reproduced or transmitted in any form or by any means without written permission from the author.

ISBN: 978-0-9829906-6-7

First Edition, May 2014
Library of Congress Control Number: 2014940519

Cover Photograph by Matthew Henry Lower

Published by *Whitest Blue Publishing*, Holland, Michigan 2014
whitestblue.com

Responses from Readers:

Thank you Shirley!! That's so encouraging! A.D., Netherlands

You are so gifted! I loved your message! Thank you for your faithfulness in sending out God's Word each week! C.W., Foley, AL

Your soliloquy today was a beautiful and colorful tapestry of vivid graphic images, exposing the heart of the Lord and the magnet of His character. N.G., Stratford-upon-Avon, England

What a blessing you are to so many! M.T., Zeeland, MI

Thank you so much for your encouraging soliloquy this week! I am so thankful that the Lord knows our needs, and He is the only one who can satisfy our emotional needs. A.L., Grand Rapids, MI

I love getting your soliloquies. Thanks for sending them. J.N. Venice, FL

Thank you, my dear friend! Mom's funeral was yesterday....print your soliloquy to read...print a copy to put in her memory book with your permission. B.E., Dalton, OH

I just read your soliloquy. Isn't it interesting that I was meditating on that same scripture just last night at work! B.H., Houston, TX

So amazing, so divine, so wonderful...that He should desire to dwell with us! B.W. Canton, OH

Loved your message and copied the link to my FB page, so others can enjoy too! Such a joy and inspiration to know you & be able to enjoy what you share from your heart! K.S., Foley, AL

Great example of living God's Word! T.F., Holland, MI

Dedicated to:

to my sisters,
Julia and Elaine,
who have been a source
of love & encouragement to me

Scripture Versions Used:

Holman Christian Standard Bible (HCSB)
King James Version (KJV)
New American Standard Bible (NASB)
New King James Version (NKJV)
New Living Translation (NLT)

Table of Contents

1. Uncertainties of Life — 401
2. A Thermometer or A Thermostat — 402
3. The Bonds That Bind — 403
4. Right in God's Sight — 404
5. Patience Wearing Thin — 405
6. Hues, Shades, & Intensity — 406
7. Drizzle & Stems — 407
8. Where Can It Be? — 408
9. A Chariot of Fire — 409

10. The Lord's Loving-kindness — 410
11. High Places — 411
12. Praising With the Psalmist — 412
13. Mountains and Valleys — 413
14. No Disappointment in Jesus — 414
15. Warm, Wonderful Feeling — 415
16. Pride Versus Humility — 416
17. "Now I Am Old" — 417
18. Hidden From View — 418
19. In What Do I Delight? — 419

20. The Foods We Eat — 420
21. Finding Peace & Happiness — 421
22. The Heavens Declare the Glory of God! — 422
23. Under His Wings — 423
24. God is Still on the Throne — 424
25. Learning From the Prophets — 425
26. Standing in the Need of Prayer — 426
27. Filled With...What? — 427
28. Travel & Reunions — 428
29. Every Knee Shall Bow — 429

30. Walking in the Light — 430

31. Praises to the Most High	431
32. Watch and Be Ready	432
33. He is Still on the Throne	433
34. The Family of God	434
35. What Terrible Timing	435
36. Am I Ready	436
37. "If That Isn't Love"	437
38. Little Baby No Longer	438
39. Through It All	439
40. The Light's Out	440
41. Pain?	441
42. Psalm 139	442
43. I Can Imagine	443
44. Jesus: A Friend Indeed!	444
45. My Wandering Mind	445
46. All That I Really Need	446
47. Casting Care Where?	447
48. "Gird Up the Mind?"	448
49. What's On My Mind?	449
50. Resting Where?	450
51. At the Top	451
52. Coming Soon!	452
53. Soaking It All Up	453
54. The Example of God's Love	454
55. Peaceful Relaxing Rest	455
56. Bless the LORD	556
57. One Step at a Time	457
58. Feelings of Rejection	458
59. Using the Scriptures	459
60. Winds of Devastating Force	460
61. "Whatever things...."	461
62. An Amazing Prayer	462
63. The Sun is Shining	463
64. Celebrating Our Liberty	464
65. A Blessed Relationship	465
66. Startling Thoughts	466

67. Receiving God's Rest	467
68. The Squirrel in the Tree	468
69. Is This God's Will?	469
70. Exercise Thyself Unto...?	470
71. Heartfelt Praise!	471
72. Similes About My LORD	472
73. God's Word...My Strength	473
74. The Music of the Earth	474
75. The Greatness of our Creator	475
76. 'Unsolvable Problems?	476
77. My Creator God Speaks!	477
78. Uncertain Future	478
79. The Faithfulness of God	479
80. A Happy Face	480
81. All Your Anxiety	481
82. Clouds	482
83. Acts of Kindness	483
84. Are You OK?	484
85. "In Everything Give Thanks"	485
86. The God of Hope	486
87. Unexpected Changes	487
88. Come to Worship Him	488
89. The Word Became Flesh	489
90. The Enormity of It All	490
91. Pause to Consider	491
92. "In This Life Only?"	492
93. The Son that Shines Forever	493
94. An Amazing Testimony	494
95. Knit Together By Love	495
96. Time Passes!	496
97. Anticipation	497
98. "God Does Not Want..."	498
99. "He Leadeth Me..."	499
100. Feelings of Inadequacy	500

*"The Lord is my shepherd;
I shall not want.
He maketh me to lie down
in green pastures:
He leadeth me
beside the still waters."
Psalm 23:1-2*

Soliloquy # 401

Uncertainties of Life

Sometimes life is full of uncertainties!
From one moment to the next,
major decisions are demanded!

My husband had prepared himself for a Total Knee Replacement that was scheduled for Monday afternoon. However on the Friday afternoon before, he was told that he needed a PET/CT Stress Test before the surgery could be approved. It was scheduled for the morning of the surgery.

'Ok,' we thought, 'We could still get to the hospital in time for surgery in the afternoon.'

So after the stress test was finished on Monday morning, we headed to the hospital in another city for his knee replacement. But during our drive there, he received a call that the surgery had been canceled, and instead he had an appointment with a cardiologist the next afternoon.

'What's going on?' I wondered. Obviously, he wouldn't know until he talked with his cardiologist. Unfortunately, he was on vacation, but an appointment was made for him on the next day with another cardiologist. However, my husband was not willing to talk with any other doctor except his own. So we needed to wait for another week until his cardiologist returned. Again I wondered, 'What is going on?'

As I pondered all these things,
I remembered that the Lord is in control.

For one thing, without the necessity of having a total knee replacement, he would never have undergone all the tests on his heart that the Orthopedic Surgeon had requested. And without all these tests, the present condition of his heart would have been known only to the Lord.

Immediately, this set our plans upside down for the time being. I was not concerned because my husband is good at taking every contingency into consideration. He always seems to have a "Plan A, and a Plan B" in mind. So he determined that we would now wait for his cardiologist to return from vacation. Then we could find out what is causing the delay with regard to the surgery on his knee and make decisions accordingly.

But I am wondering: Will we be staying here in case his heart needs attention, or will we be returning north to our home? If we should have to return north, what preparations must I be making before we leave?

Oh, the uncertainties of life!
There is no guarantee that everything
will remain the same
from one moment to the next.

The Bible states this in language that is "pelucidly plain." (quoting my husband's oft repeated phrase!) This is especially true with respect to the most important decision of all: The issue of salvation: The question everyone needs to answer is:

'Where will I spend eternity?"
If that question has never been answered,
it must be decided now,
TODAY!

Behold now is the accepted time
Behold now is the day of salvation.
2 Corinthians 6:2 (KJV)

Soliloquy # 402

A Thermometer or A Thermostat?

Am I like a thermometer or a thermostat?
That is quite a question!

My husband and I went to hear the president of a Bible College recently. His message touched my heart in several ways. But when he spoke about the differences between a thermometer and a thermostat, it grabbed my attention. As a result that concept has stayed in my mind.

He spoke about the week between the triumphal entry of Jesus into Jerusalem and eventually to His crucifixion. At the beginning of that week, the crowd cut branches from trees and spread them on the road Others spread their garments on the road. Still others went before Him crying out,

Hosanna to the Son of David;
Blessed is He who comes in the name of the Lord;
Hosanna in the highest!
Matthew 21:8-9

What a sight that must have been! It would certainly have excited a crowd so that they would want to see what was going on. It could be that many of them had already seen his miracles, how the blind had received their sight, and how the lame had walked again. They had probably heard how He walked on the water, calmed the sea, and even called Lazarus from the dead!

But they were not the only ones who had heard about these things!

The elders and religious leaders were becoming increasingly concerned about this phenomenon. They were not pleased, for had not Jesus criticized them saying they were "whited sepulchres, full of dead men's bones?" Jesus had told them that they put on an outward appearance, but their hearts were far from God.

Yes, they'd heard plenty about Him. Were they jealous or afraid of their positions? All they knew was that Jesus couldn't be allowed to continue or their positions would be in jeopardy.

So only a few days later, they used Judas to betray Jesus so they could have him arrested and put on trial. At the trial, the Bible states that the chief priests and the elders *persuaded* the multitudes to ask for Jesus to be put to death (Matthew 27:20-23)!

Did they not set the atmosphere – the thermostat - so that the crowd followed? Yes, the crowds were reflecting the temperature that the thermostat had set.

I wondered if perhaps the crowds had not even realized that He was the One to whom they were shouting their praises just a few days earlier?

> They were swayed by the thermostat that the leaders had set.
> They felt the temperature and acted accordingly!

So the profound question that struck me is: 'Am I simply going along with the temperature of the crowd?' Or, 'Can I be a thermostat that will make a difference in someone's life today?'

> *Be thou an example of the believers,*
> *in word, in conversation,*
> *in charity, in spirit,*
> *in faith, in purity.*
> *1 Timothy 4:12*

Soliloquy # 403

The Bonds That Bind

The trip north seemed almost endless this year.

As I think about it, it did take us three days because we wanted to stop in Tennessee to visit with my dear 86 year old sister, her husband, and in-laws. It was good seeing her smiling face once again. We appreciated visiting with the family and enjoying their kindness and their help.

Perhaps another reason the trip seemed longer was because of my husband's distress with his knee. As long as we were sitting, it didn't seem to bother him as much. But whenever we had to stop and get out of the car, he felt quite handicapped, gritting his teeth trying to bear the pain.

As we were driving into our city, I excitedly called my dear younger sister to tell her. She said that she and her husband would be right over! And they did come with bran muffins she had made and also oranges they'd brought back from Florida. They both helped unload the car, as I started putting things away. Then we had a cup of tea together, catching up on news. It was good spending time with them!

Now we await my husband's appointment with the cardiologist this week who needs to give his "OK" for the Orthopedic Surgeon to do the total knee replacement. That cannot come soon enough for him!

Recently, I realized how dependent we all are on others. How awful it would be to feel *alone* during these times in our lives! I'm grateful beyond words for all our family and our many dear friends who enrich our lives in so many ways. The oneness we all have because of our common love of the Lord Jesus Christ forms a strong bond that cannot be broken, for it is an eternal one. The hymn-writer said it so well, *Blest Be the Tie that Binds our hearts in Christian love.*

I thought of the "bonds" mentioned in the Bible. For example, Hosea 11:4 talks about the Lord leading with "bonds of love" (NAS). The apostle Paul talks about the "bond of peace." He exhorts believers to,

*walk in a manner worthy of the calling
with which you have been called,*

*with all humility and gentleness,
with patience,
showing forbearance to one another in love,*

*being diligent to preserve
the unity of the spirit in the **bond of peace**.
Ephesians 4:1-3*

Paul considered himself to be a
"bond-servant of Christ Jesus"
and also "of God"
(Romans 1:1; Titus 1:1).

He also willingly considered himself
as a bond-servant for Jesus' sake to the believers
(2 Corinthians 4:5).

Thank you, Lord, for experiencing
these many bonds that bind those
who are your children together!

Soliloquy # 404

Right in God's Sight

After the many times that I read...

He did evil in the sight of the LORD....
He did evil in the sight of the LORD....
He did evil in the sight of the LORD....

...it was truly refreshing to read that Hezekiah
did right in the sight of the LORD.

I almost had to breathe a sigh of relief,
for it was depressing to read in the book of Second Kings
about all the evil that the kings were doing
continually in the sight of the LORD.

Then when I came to the 18th chapter
and read that Hezekiah, king of Judah,
"did right in the sight of the LORD,"
it was almost like a breath of fresh air
and a ray of sunshine!

The record went on to explain that,

..He trusted in the LORD, the God of Israel,
so that after him there was none like him
among all the kings of Judah,
nor among those who were before him.

For he clung to the LORD,
he did not depart from following Him,
but kept his commandments,
which the LORD had commanded Moses.

And the LORD was with him;
wherever he went he prospered.

2 Kings 18:5-7

How wonderful that he left such an epitaph so that it was recorded
for future centuries that he was a king worthy to be remembered!

Even though some of those other kings did some things
that were good in their own eyes for Israel and Judah,
the LORD their God had commanded them
in no uncertain terms through Moses
and through other prophets
exactly what would happen
if they did not obey His commandments.

And what was prophesied did eventually happen.

And does not the Lord also want the same
from His children today?

The Bible tells us that some will say,
Lord, have we not done this and done that in your name?

But He will say,
*Depart from me, ye workers of iniquity,
I never knew you.*

Just because something seems good in one's own eyes,
that doesn't mean it is right in God's sight!
(Matthew 7:21-23).

How wonderful to be able to hear in that last day,

Well done, thou good and faithful servant!

Soliloquy # 405

Patience Wearing Thin!

My patience is wearing thin, and I don't like the feeling.
I feel as though my nerves are stretched tight
as a rubber band, ready to snap!
I'm not used to this at all!

It was several days ago that my husband and I were in the Emergency room at the hospital. He had been having chest discomfort for a couple days, so he felt the need to have it checked out as its intensity had been increasing. Since he has had a history of heart problems, the hospital Emergency room takes this quite seriously. After a number of doctors and tests, they admitted him and continued testing into the next day. This culminated in a heart catherization. Naturally I didn't want to leave him in case he needed anything, so I spent Sunday and Monday nights in a chair next to him. At times during the night I had to help him untangle from the IV tubes that were in his arm or get him water or whatever he needed. Most everything in his heart had checked out OK, although a valve was in question. So Tuesday, before he was discharged, the doctor ordered another Echocardiogram to compare with the one that had been done a month before. He wanted to check those results with the previous one. Any significant difference might help diagnose his problems.

Yes, that was a bit tiring and stressful, but the next day, Wednesday, I had an appointment that I had to keep with a dermatologist to check a couple of spots on my hand and neck. They were becoming rough and irritated. The dermatologist thought they looked suspicious and did a biopsy of both of them and sent them away. Now they are even more of a continual irritation to me.

So probably the lack of sleep, the increased irritation of my neck and top of my hand, and also an irritation on my right eyelid are part of the culprits that are causing me extra vexation.

I thought, 'Oh yes! Vexation! King Saul called for David to play on his harp when he was vexed in his spirit!' I haven't been home to be able to play on my little harp. Come to think of it, now my husband is taking a nap, so I can't disturb him at the present time either.

Well, I'm not used to this at all, so I went to the Lord in prayer. Then I felt led to write and search in the Bible about a lack of patience.

2 Corinthians 6:3-6 urges believers to give no cause for offense in anything so that the ministry will not be discredited! Instead we must endure all afflictions. It even mentions sleeplessness! And then in verse 6, the apostle Paul mentions, *in purity, in knowledge, in **patience**, in kindness...."*

The familiar passage naming the fruit of the Spirit came back to me, but I felt I needed to check those fruits using my modern English Bible. I found they really hit home in that version. I will need to add them to my bathroom mirror so that they will often be before me. Thank you Lord, for Your Word and Your presence, especially in these days when my patience is wearing thin!

But the fruit of the Spirit is love, joy, peace,
***patience**, kindness, goodness,*
faithfulness, gentleness, self-control,
against such things there is no law.
Galatians 5:22-23 (NASB)

Soliloquy #406

Hues, Shades, & Intensity

I was looking outside
at the trees just starting to fill out with leaves.

All of a sudden the differences in the shades of them,
the various hues and intensities,
even the shadows on some of them,
seemed to come alive with greater variegation.

I remembered especially when I was a child, I didn't notice such things. When asked, "What color are the trees?" I would invariably answer, "They are green!" It wasn't until I was older that I began to notice the different hues, shades and intensities of colors. And that opened up a new world to me.

I realized that,
the young leaves were slightly different
from the ones farther open.
The different types of trees had different shades of green.
They all contrasted with the greens of the nearby bushes.
Even the grass had multiple shades of green.

'Wow,' I thought, 'What a great artist our Creator God is!'
I'm so thankful for His excellence in His creation.
It fills me with a deep appreciation and pleasure.

I thought of the hymn-writer George W. Robinson, 1876, who had marveled over God's creation also.

When he became Christian and had communion with the Lord, everything seemed to take on more vibrancy. He wrote the beautiful, heart-warming words to the hymn, *I Am His and He is Mine*.

> "Heav'n above is softer blue,
> Earth around is sweeter green!
> Something lives in every hue
> Christ-less eyes have never seen;
> Birds with gladder songs o'erflow,
> flowers with deeper beauties shine,
> Since I know, as now I know,
> I am His, and He is mine."

It is interesting how one's spirit is revived because of having a personal relationship with the Lord Jesus Christ. It seems that everything can be enjoyed to a greater degree.

The Psalmist wrote:

> *It is good to give thanks to the Lord,*
> *and to sing praises to Thy name, O Most High;*
>
> *To declare Thy loving-kindness in the morning,*
> *And Thy faithfulness by night,*
> *With the ten-stringed lute and with the harp;*
> *With resounding music upon the lyre.*
>
> *For Thou, O LORD, has made me glad*
> *by what Thou hast done,*
> *I will sing for joy at the works of Thy hands.*
> *Psalm 92:1-4*

Soliloquy # 407

Drizzle & Stems

Drizzle and Stems!

Our four year old great-grandson came from Ohio for a visit to take in the activities of Tulip Time with his Mom and Grandma (our daughter). But the rain and drizzle didn't seem to dampen his vivacious spirit for a minute! Instead each day, he eagerly looked forward to everything he saw around him.

He did seem to look with a very serious expression at the stems that were remaining of many of the tulips, but whenever we did see some tulips in full bloom, he would be visibly impressed!

Evidently there had been so much hot weather in the month of March, that many flowers and plants began their growth spurts prematurely. Therefore many of the tulips that would normally be in perfect bloom at this time, were well past that stage.

However, there were many other activities going on everywhere, so none of these things bothered our great-grandson! He would simply continue bouncing along holding his mother's or grandmother's hands.

> I began thinking about the trusting spirit of young children.
> How wonderful it is to see!
> The absolute faith that he had in his Mom and Grandma
> made it possible for him to be willing
> to do and see everything that they decided.
> He even happily went along shopping with them.
> They figured that since there was so much rain and drizzle,
> it seemed the best way to get a break from it
> -- besides the merchants had enticing sales advertised!

It all reminded me of the little children's chorus we used to sing,

The birdies in the treetops sing their song,
The angels chant their chorus all day long,
The flowers in the garden blend their hue,
So why shouldn't I, why shouldn't you,
Praise Him too?

Yes, indeed!
"Why shouldn't I, why shouldn't you, praise Him too?"

We should take more notice of these precious little children who are so filled with excitement and awe over all the things they see -- even though it might be a festival of stems and drizzle.

The Lord Jesus Christ, when He was on earth, certainly took notice of the little children. When His disciples rebuked the people for bringing the children to Him, He was 'indignant' and said to them,

Permit the children to come to Me;

do not hinder them;
for the kingdom of God belongs to such as these.

Truly I say to you,
whoever does not receive the kingdom of God
like a child shall not enter it at all.
Mark 10:14-15 (NASB)

Soliloquy # 408

Where Can It Be?

I have looked high and low all over our little home,
but the canopy cover for our porch swing seems to be missing!

Since the sun is shining brightly and warming everything up, I am eager to be able to sit out there enjoying a cup of coffee in the morning. However since I've had biopsies on some spots on my skin, I should be protected from the bright sun.

But, alas, my husband and I have looked all over our small condo. But it just seems to have disappeared! I think, 'It must be around here somewhere!' But it is not to be found.

There is one good thing that is coming out of our predicament and that is that our little condo is getting a good cleaning. Hopefully we will be donating some of the items that we haven't used for a while to the local Bibles for Mexico thrift store.

Yes, that is all good. Yet, our canopy cover still seems to be lost!

I thought of the parable of Jesus that is recorded in Luke 15:2-10. The Pharisees and the scribes were always grumbling about something or other about Jesus. This time they were saying, *"This man receives sinners and eats with them."* So Jesus told them some parables. One of my favorites is the parable of the lost sheep. In fact we have a beautiful picture of *"The Lost Sheep"* in our Family Room.

What man among you,
if he has a hundred sheep
and has lost one of them,
does not leave the ninety-nine in the open pasture,
and go after the one which is lost, until he finds it?
And when he has found it,

he lays it on his shoulders, rejoicing,
And when he comes home,
he calls together his friends and his neighbors,
saying to them,
'Rejoice with me,
for I have found my sheep which was lost.'

I tell you that in the same way,
there will be more joy in heaven
over one sinner who repents,
than over ninety-nine righteous persons
who need no repentance.
Luke 15:4-7 (NASB)

How beautiful!
How kind and loving!
How compassionate!
It touches my heart!

Jesus said that He came
to seek and to save those that were lost. (Matthew 18:11)
Each person is important in God's sight.
He doesn't want even one to be lost!

So getting back to the canopy cover for the porch swing,
I'd better start looking again.
Oh yes, there will certainly be rejoicing
when I finally find it!

Soliloquy # 409

A Chariot of Fire

When I heard that our long-time fellow laborer and dear friend, Vernon Anderson, had gone to be with the Lord, the indelible image that came into my mind was of the Lord's comforting arms welcoming him. But then the image expanded and I could not shake it from my mind. It kept growing....

It was an image where I felt as if I were with him as he bowed humbly before the Lord in worship and praise. I felt his heart going out to the Lord as he thanked Him for His continual hand upon his life and that of his beloved wife, Darlene, and their children; for the way in which He had answered their prayers and kept His hand of protection upon them; for His miraculous intervention in their lives through so many difficult circumstances all over the world. Yes, He had continually provided for their needs, many times above what they asked or even thought (Ephesians 3:20).

Then the images from the book of the Revelation came to mind, and I visualized Vernon being privileged to join with the "myriads of myriads, and thousands of thousands" who were worshiping and saying in a mighty chorus:

> *Worthy is the Lamb that was slain*
> *to receive power and riches and wisdom*
> *and might and honor and glory and blessing.*
> *Revelation 5:12 (NASB)*

After that, I thought of him being reunited with their daughter, Laurel, who had died so long ago at 12 years of age shortly after they had arrived in the Philippine Islands. I thought of their heartache and the criticism of so many because they had taken their young children to a foreign land. Yes, I imagined the two of them standing hand in hand, joining in the worship of their Lord and Savior. But then I saw thousands -- thousands upon thousands

-- joining them who had come to know the Savior through the influence of their ministry in so many lands.

What a wonderful homecoming that would have been for him! He was truly a pioneer in missions. His unquenchable zeal for opening a witness in many countries around the world became a reality. But he realized the need for the training of the nationals so that they could lead their own people. So he got Bible training centers established in many countries. He had a burden for the nations that lay heavy upon his heart from the time when he became a Christian and gave up his business to train and give his life to the service of the Lord until his dying day.

Yes, he was one who could have joined with those caught up in Chariots of Fire for he also was one who led in the advancement of the gospel to the nations (2 Kings 2:11; 6:17; and 13:14).

...there appeared a chariot of fire and horses of fire which separated the two of them. And Elijah went up by a whirlwind to heaven. 2 Kings 2:11;

Elisha prayed and said, "O Lord, I pray, open his eyes that he may see." And the LORD opened the servant's eyes, and he saw; and behold, the mountain was full of horses and chariots of fire all around Elisha. 6:17;

When Elisha became sick with the illness of which he was to die, Joash the king of Israel came down to him and wept over him and said, "My father, my father, the chariots of Israel and its horsemen!" 13:14.

Vern was indeed a chariot of fire!

Soliloquy # 410

The Lord's Loving-kindness

How interesting that during the past week, a number of people have asked me about my husband's knee surgery. They were wondering how he was recovering.

That brought back to mind the images over the last half a year how he could hardly walk, even with a cane or walker. He was desperate to have surgery, but the doctor in southern Alabama had canceled it due to the condition of his heart. Besides an EKG, Echocardiogram, PET/CT Stress Test, he now needed a catherization. So we headed north to Michigan to see what could be done there.

However, a few days after arriving home, he awoke on a Saturday morning with discomfort in his chest, so he rested on the sofa. After a while, he got up and was amazed that his knee didn't hurt any longer! All throughout the day, his chest bothered him, but he had relief from the excruciating pain in his knee! Strangely that continued on through Sunday.

Late in the evening, we went to the emergency in the hospital, because his chest discomfort was getting worse. He was examined thoroughly by several doctors. The pain disappearing from his knee had them puzzled, so they checked for a possibility of a blood clot going from the knee into the chest, but those tests were negative. His cardiologist did a heart catherization, but it showed no significant change from the one that was done several years before. So after a couple of days and nights in the hospital, he was discharged.

Yes, indeed! How interesting! The medical profession had no answers. But I knew the Lord had been merciful to him granting him relief from that pain, and I still keep thanking Him!

'Oh..., but the Lord doesn't work that way anymore today,' I hear some people saying. 'Didn't the apostle Paul have to leave Trophimus sick at Miletus? Didn't he tell Timothy to take a little wine for his stomach's sake and his oft infirmities? Didn't Paul, himself, have a 'thorn in the flesh' that he begged the Lord to take away? But instead the Lord told him that His grace would be sufficient!'

I agree. 'That is all true. But nevertheless, God is still God!
And He is still on the Throne.
If He desires to put His hand of healing on someone,
certainly He is able!'

This has proven to be true in my own life.
How can I help but praise Him for His mercy
and His loving-kindness!

Along with the Psalmist, my song is,

*But Thou, O LORD,
art a God merciful and gracious,
Slow to anger and abundant in
loving-kindness and truth....*

*"I will sing of the loving-kindness
of the LORD forever,
To all generations I will make known
Thy faithfulness with my mouth.
Psalm 86:15; 89:1 (NASB)*

Soliloquy # 411

High Places

I just received an heart-wrenching email from a friend asking for prayer for her husband. She went into detail about what had been done in the hospital to try to offset the melanoma that was attacking him.

As she told about the doctors taking skin from his back to graft onto the spot, my nerves almost stood on edge. I could feel the pain, and it was definitely not comfortable! This was probably due to the fact that I have been struggling with the effects of "chemo creme" that I'm having to apply to my own skin.

Recently I have been reading a book, *Leaders Who Made A Difference* by Paul W. Chappell. It has been proving a blessing, but also a challenge. He cites three great leaders in the Bible: Joshua, Nehemiah, and Joseph. About 78% of the way through the book, I read the following quote, and it seemed to really hit home:

> *Anyone can be faithful when the sun is shining*
> *and life feels grand,*
> *but it is faithfulness through the dark nights*
> *and lonely valleys that proves genuine faith.*
>
> *A faith that cannot be tested cannot be trusted,*
> *so God often tests our faith.*
> *If the test reveals continued faithfulness to God,*
> *our faith brings glory to God*
> *and honors Him in the eyes of all who observe the test.*

How true it is that when the sun is shining and all is going well, it's easy to trust! However, when hard times hit, it would be so easy to quit and fall back on some "crutch" to help endure the hardship. But would that be "passing the test?" Or would I be sliding along or even going backward?

I thought of the thought-provoking allegory in the book by Hannah Hurnard, *Hind's Feet on High Places*. Hannah's allegory follows "Much-Afraid" as she goes on her difficult journey with her two companions "Sorrow and Suffering." She keeps striving toward the "high places," but her path is often very difficult. Though tempted to find an easier way, she persisted until she reached the "high places." This little book made an impact in my life and continues to do so even today.

I thought how true it seems to be that the times of sorrow and suffering are so often the means of getting me to higher ground in the knowledge of my wonderful, compassionate, and loving Savior.

The Lord God is my strength,
And He has made my feet like hinds' feet,
And makes me walk on my high places.
Habakkuk 3:19

As Johnson Oatman Jr. (1856-1926) wrote,

I'm pressing on the upward way,
New heights I'm gaining every day;
Still praying as I onward bound,
Lord, plant my feet on higher ground.

May my faith bring glory to God,
no matter what the test might be.
May He lead me on to higher ground.

Soliloquy # 412

Praising With the Psalmist

The book of Psalms!
What blessings I experienced!
I couldn't stop reading them this morning!
Besides the fact that they are considered spiritual poetry,
they seemed to reflect what is in my heart.

It is good to give thanks to the LORD,
And to sing praises to Thy name, O Most High;
To declare Thy loving-kindness in the morning,
And Thy faithfulness by night...
For Thou, O LORD, hast made me glad
by what Thou has done,
I will sing for joy at the works of Thy hands.
Psalm 92:1-2,4

I thought to myself,
'What a perfect time to be reading these heart-touching words!'
During this past week,
there have been several friends
who have been in my prayers.
They had surgeries with positive results.
How grateful I am for the loving-kindness of the LORD!

My own daughter has been uppermost in my mind,
for she had a heart catherization.
After changes in medications,
her vital signs have seemed to be stabilized.

Then also, my son, grandson, and granddaughter
were attending training seminars
for their places of employment.
They were in three different cities:
Houston, Boston, and Cleveland.

So they were all in my prayers
and placed in the Lord's mighty hands.

*The righteous man will flourish
like the palm tree,...
like a cedar....*

*They will still yield fruit in old age;
They shall be full of sap and very green,
To declare that the LORD is upright;*

*He is my rock,
and there is no unrighteousness in Him.
Psalm 92:12, 14-15*

It's true that the LORD is not limited
to just one occasion or to one person.
His mighty hand is evident in many different places,
even though their needs might be different!

Indeed, from the bottom of my heart,
following the Psalmist,
I praise the LORD:

*How great are Thy works, O LORD!
Thy thoughts are very deep.
Psalm 92:5*

Thank You, O LORD, my God, and my Rock!

Soliloquy # 413

Mountains and Valleys

It is exhilarating to go up to the top of a mountain.
The view is magnificent!
I have to exclaim,
'What a great Creator we have,
His artistry is unbelievable!'

But then, there needs to be a descent again into the valley
before another mountain can be climbed.

How like life that often seems to be! After some wonderful and inspiring experience either alone or with others, there comes a "let down."

'Well,' I thought to myself, 'It probably wouldn't be good to stay on top all the time. There needs to be a time in the valley.' As the song writer said, "For the God of the mountain is still God in the valley."

Then my mind went to some of the leading people in the Bible.
For example,

Joseph rose to the highest position possible,
yet he ended up in prison.

Moses was on the mountain top with God,
but when he went down,
the people were worshiping an idol.

David had attained the position as the king of Israel,
yet when he was tested, he fell.

From the heights,
to some of the lowest depths they fell.

Yes, it seems that being on the physical mountain top can be exhilarating, but I realize that it is not possible to stay there. There has to be a descent some time.

Is it not the same in the emotional realm? Most people feel the "highs" and "lows" of experiences. How is it possible to deflect the stress of the valley after being on a mountain top experience?

Once again, I sought God's Word for the answer. Could the key be to fix my eyes on Jesus as my example. He promised to be with me at all times (Hebrews 13:5).

*Let us run with patience
the race that is set before us.*

*Looking unto Jesus
the author and finisher of our faith;
who for the joy that was set before him
endured the cross, despising the shame,
and is set down at the right hand
of the throne of God.*
Hebrews 12:1-2 (KJV)

Soliloquy # 414

No Disappointment in Jesus

There's no disappointment in Jesus
He's more than my tongue can tell,
His love is so sure and so steadfast,
His friendship divine will not fail.

There's no disappointment in Jesus,
Tho' sorrows may press me sore;
He comforts with tender compassion,
His love cheers my heart evermore.

There's no disappointment in Jesus.
He's all that he promised to be;
His love and His care comfort me everywhere,
He is no disappointment to me.
--John C. Hallett, 1940

This wonderful song came into my mind this afternoon
and brought great comfort to me.

I had been proofing my husband's manuscript for days, all day long, every day. I was really pushing myself because I was eager to get it to the publisher.

Finally! I had finished the last page! Ah! The tremendous burden lifted as I joyously wrote a note to the publisher and sent the MSS.

But alas! When I checked it, none of the corrections were there!

It was as if I had done NOTHING! All 257 pages of it had no corrections on them! Then the disabling disappointment set in!

I didn't feel like doing a thing! Nothing! I was beat!

I went into the kitchen, and got an orange,
after all it was 5:30 already.
But still the disappointment didn't leave me.

My recliner beckoned me,
and I stretched out on it with my orange in my hand.

Then the wonderful song by John Hallett entered my mind.
It wouldn't leave!
I felt all my disabling disappointment leave me
as I began to rejoice in the fact
that there is NO disappointment in Jesus!
And I sincerely thanked Him!

I decided that I would leave
my husband's manuscript
until later next week.

Then I remembered that my daughter and granddaughter will be arriving from Ohio. So that put the final lid on the disappointment! I will be ready to begin it again after they leave.

Meanwhile,
I rejoice in the Lord's presence
and help in my time of need.

Come unto me, all ye that labour
and are heavy laden,
and I will give you rest.
Matthew 11:28

Soliloquy # 415

Warm, Wonderful Feeling

Instead of a dismal 'let-down' feeling,
I'm on the mountain top once again.
I'm thanking the Lord for my family and all my friends,
I'm thanking the One Who makes such blessings possible.

It started with my granddaughter and her friend coming from Ohio for a visit. She enjoyed a few days of sharing our area and places where I had taken her when she was younger. Evidently she must still hold fond memories in her mind. But it was time for them to leave, so sadly we waved 'good-bye.'

Shortly after they left, my husband received a call from the dear pastor of our former church. He and his family were in our area for a little vacation. During the time they were around here, we were able to go out to dinner a couple times, and also spent wonderful hours of good fellowship with them. However, before they left to go back to Ohio, the special times did not end...

For our daughter, her four year old grandson and his mommy came for a fun-filled visit! They visited the beach, the community pool, a couple of parks, had a picnic with our daughter's aunts and cousins enjoying a pot-luck meal with them. They saw various attractions in the area, including the holiday fireworks! But it seems that all things must come to an end, so sadly, we had to say 'good-bye.'

However, it still didn't end! For shortly after they left for Ohio, our neighborhood had a special celebration for the Fourth of July. They had placed small American flags about 10 feet apart all along the roads. Also many residents had flags flying from their homes. It looked quite patriotic. They had prepared hot dogs, potato salad, pork & beans, cole slaw, and ice cream drumsticks for dessert! It was good to renew acquaintances with our neighbors and meet people who had recently moved here.

All in all, it has been an extremely full, fun-filled, and heart-warming week! So this evening, though being a bit tired, I have warm wonderful feelings in my heart! 'But alas,' I thought to myself, 'How often do such experiences result in a crash, a getting back down-to-earth experience!'

And that's exactly what took place, for my dishwasher 'gave up the ghost!' Unfortunately, it happened while the family was still here. Though disappointing, we simply went back to the 'old-fashioned' way of doing the dishes! Yes, it brought back many memories, but yet it also made me realize how very fortunate I am to be living where there was a built-in dishwasher. Probably most people do not have that luxury. I realized how easy it is to take things like that for granted.

So this morning I am grateful: grateful for having many friends and for my loving family; grateful for living in a country where we can celebrate our country's birthday and heritage of freedom; grateful for the modern conveniences that I often take for granted; and especially grateful that I can read my Bible and worship the Lord. So, instead of a 'let-down' feeling, I still have the Lord Who, as the Psalmist says, continues to be my lamp lighting my darkness!

But Thou dost light my lamp;
The Lord my God illumines my darkness.
Psalm 18:28

Soliloquy #416

Pride Verses Humility

I wish I could remember more of my dream....
But somehow, when I awoke,
all I knew was that it had something to do with pride.
As a result, that subject
has been flitting around my mind all week.

I began to think of the number of people who seem to be compelled to tear others down. Is it because they need to build themselves up? Is it because they have insecure feelings themselves and feel that it is necessary to put others down so that they might look better? Or could it be because of pride?

What would be the possible consequences of such prideful behavior? It must hurt deeply and leave feelings of inferiority and insecurity. My heart aches, and I cringe when I think about it.

The Bible urges a person to esteem others as being better than one's self. Philippians 2:3 says,

> *Let nothing be done through strife or vainglory:*
> *but in lowliness of mind*
> *let each esteem other*
> *better than themselves.*

How pleasant it would be to live in a place where people do this. There would be no room for pride or an "haughty spirit." Though Proverbs 16:18 is oft-quoted, the end of the verse is often neglected.

> *Pride goeth before destruction,*
> *and an haughty spirit before a fall.*

Many kings in the Old Testament were examples of this: When they were in dire need, they sought the Lord their God; and God won battles for them and blessed them. But after a while, they became proud and started boasting in all their success as if they themselves had produced the things that God had given them. The result? "They fell!" And the fall was often very great and humbling.

The Bible says that all those things were written to be examples. 1 Corinthians 10:11 states that,

Now all these things happened unto them
for ensamples:
and they are written for our admonition....
1 Corinthians 10:11

Even today, there are people who are achieving great things and tend to forget James 1:17,

Every good gift and every perfect gift is from above,
and cometh down from the Father of lights...

"A word to the wise is sufficient."

May I always remember this fact
and also that,

...GOD RESISTETH THE PROUD,
BUT GIVETH GRACE TO THE HUMBLE.
James 4:6

Soliloquy # 417

Now I am Old

Musing about my trip tomorrow
to see my older sister and her husband,
I began thinking about life in general.

It does seem that it sometimes becomes more complicated as a person gets older. Often there is a greater need of more care and even assistance in mundane matters. It might even become necessary to relinquish decisions and leave them to others. It must be difficult for one, who in years past was totally independent, to find that he or she has to depend on others.

In the case of my sister, she has led an active life. She has taught at Christian colleges and has been a guest speaker at various functions. She touched many lives, young as well as old. So, even though she cannot be active any longer, her legacy continues on through many lives.

However, even in her present circumstances in which she now finds herself, I know she would say that the Lord does not fail. She would say along with King David (Psalm 37:25),

I have been young, and now am old;
yet have I not seen the righteous forsaken.

King David lived a full life
and knew about the infirmities of the aged.
Yet he gave good advice,

Delight thyself also in the Lord,
and He shall give thee the desires of thine heart.

Commit thy way unto the Lord;
trust also in Him;

and He shall bring it to pass.
Psalm 37:4-5

Many times I have proven these Scriptures to be true!
King David's son, King Solomon, said,

Trust in the LORD with all thine heart;
and lean not unto thine own understanding.
In all thy ways acknowledge Him,
and He shall direct thy paths.
Proverbs 3:5-6

What a comfort to know,
that even though I might grow old and become infirm,
the Lord remains in control
and He continues to direct my path!

The prophet Isaiah wrote about the resulting peace,

Thou wilt keep Him in perfect peace,
whose mind is stayed upon Thee:
because he trusteth in Thee.
Isaiah 26:3

Soliloquy # 418

Hidden from View

How insidious some things can be!

For example:
A fairly small spot or irritation on the skin
can hold unknown surprises underneath.

After having had a biopsy that revealed basal cell carcinoma on my neck, I was instructed to apply "chemo cream" on the affected area. That was just fine for a while, but that spot appeared to be spreading, and that didn't seem right to me! It wasn't supposed to spread, it was supposed to make it better, not worse! However the dermatologist said that the "Aldara" didn't affect normal skin, but it worked on any cancerous cells that might be around it, and so it was taking care of the rest of them that weren't visible on the surface.

'Interesting,' I thought,
'Kinda' like a good looking apple that appears perfect.
But one bite into it shows a browning or rotten area inside of it!'

Thankfully some make-up can hide blemishes
that would otherwise make the skin look blotchy.

A potter can form a bowl
that might be quite useless in everyday cooking
even though it might look good on the surface.

Good on the outside, inside rotten? Jesus even called the religious leaders, "Whited sepulchers, full of dead man's bones."

Jesus quoted the prophecy of Isaiah (29:13)
when he accused the religious leaders of his day
:
These people honor me with their lips,

but their hearts are far from me.
Matthew 15:8

The Bible does warn that,

*The Word of God is quick, and powerful,
and sharper than any two-edged sword,
piercing even to the dividing asunder of soul and spirit,
and of the joints and marrow,
and is a discerner of the thoughts
and intents of the heart.*
Hebrews 4:12

It sounds like God's Word is a little bit like the Aldara cream, revealing the disease under the surface, hidden from view.

So it would be well to prepare for that day
when all people's secrets will be revealed.
It would therefore be wise to follow
the advice of the Psalmist:

*Search me, O God, and know my heart:
try me, and know my thoughts:
and see if there be any wicked way in me,
and lead me in the way everlasting.*
Psalm 139:23-24

Soliloquy #419

In What Do I Delight?

What are the things in which I take great delight?
That question came to me the other day as I read Jeremiah 9:24,

> *But the one who boasts should boast in this,*
> *that he understands and knows Me –*
> *that I am the LORD showing faithful love,*
> *justice, and righteousness on the earth,*
> *for I delight in these things.*
> *Jeremiah 9:24 (HCSB)*

It was intriguing to me that the LORD takes delight in such things! So I paused to consider the question again, 'What are the things in which I take great delight?'

Well, the first thing that popped into my mind
was the thought of seeing my children and grandchildren
when they come to visit.
The welling up of warmth and tears of joy
as I look at the sparkle in their eyes
cannot be compared to much else!
Or whenever I hear of something special
that they have accomplished,
or when things are going well for them,
these bring much pleasure to me.

Since the Olympics are presently dominating the news, the faces of the athletes, or the pride evidenced on the faces of their parents and loved ones, indicate that they harbor similar feelings at their great accomplishments. But surely there had to have been failures along the way.

So when I read in the Psalms
that the LORD takes pleasure or delights in certain ways,

I thought of the athletes and their parents.

How appropriate are the words penned by the Psalmist.
He stated that even when a person falls
no feelings of failure
need overtake and discourage him,
because,

*A man's steps are established by the LORD,
and He takes pleasure in his way.
Though he falls, he will not be overwhelmed,
because the LORD holds his hand.
Psalm 37:23-24*

Even when there were times of disappointment
over the behavior of the remnant of God's people,
Micah asked the following question of God,

*Who is a God like You,
removing iniquity and passing over rebellion
for the remnant of His inheritance?
He does not hold on to His anger forever,
because He delights in faithful love.
Micah 7:18*

Soliloquy # 420

The Foods We Eat

My sister and I went pickin' blueberries this morning.

It was a perfect morning,
not as hot and humid as it had been.
The skies were blue with white clouds overhead,
and the blueberry bushes were still wet from the irrigation.

We were told that it was the last week for pickin'.
We noticed that the berries were smaller
and it took us longer to get the quantity we had a week ago,
but we were satisfied.
We had enough for our purposes:
my husband and I enjoy eating them
with our cereal in the morning;
and my sister makes the best pies
a person could wish to eat!

Oh, the blessings of being able to live in an area where things like this are possible. In the past we have also picked strawberries and peaches. Fresh cherries were available, and later on we can visit the apple orchard. These wonderful fruits are delicious treats.

My thoughts went back to my daughter who has been suffering with great pain, especially in her wrists, elbows, and feet; well, just about all over. Often the pain would wake her at night. So she decided to do research on the computer to find foods that might help to reduce the pain.

Interestingly, she found that kale and turmeric were foods known for reducing inflammation. So she stopped on the way home from work to get them. She added other vegetables to her salad, and decided it was really good! Since the article suggested eating less sugar, she has also stopped eating cookies, cakes, and desserts, hoping that something would help to reduce the inflammation.

The next day when she was at work, she realized that her pain had greatly lessened to the extent that she didn't even wear her wrist and elbow braces. She was quite amazed!

So throughout the week, she kept eating a salad of those veggies each day and refraining from consuming sugar. Amazingly, she still hasn't been experiencing that unbearable pain. She can hardly believe it! She told me she was going to cancel the appointment that she had with the doctor tomorrow.

> I thought how interesting it is that all those natural things
> that grow in the earth are good for people;
> and so many things that people have made
> and processed are harmful!

> Sometimes it seems that my diet has degenerated
> into consuming many processed foods,
> and quite often even fast foods.

> I must remember that God does know best!
> He has given us the good earth
> where these beneficial foods grow.
> It is so easy, yet oftentimes it seems so hard.

The Bible says,

> *For every creature of God is good,*
> *and nothing to be refused,*
> *if it be received with thanksgiving.*
> *1 Timothy 4:4*

Soliloquy # 421

Finding Peace & Happiness

Why is it that so many people
seem to be discontented so much of the time?
They seem to be constantly searching for something,
but they really don't know what.
The question is,

'Where can a person find peace and happiness?'

Whenever I am troubled over this question,
I know that the Bible has the answer.
Philippians 4:4-8 in the New American Standard Bible reads:

Rejoice in the Lord always;
again I will say, rejoice!
Let your forbearing spirit be known to all men.
The Lord is near.

Be anxious for nothing,
but in everything by prayer and supplication
with thanksgiving
let your requests
be made known to God.

And the peace of God,
which surpasses all comprehension,
shall guard your hearts and your minds
in Christ Jesus.

Finally, brethren,
whatever is true,
whatever is honorable,
whatever is right,

> *whatever is pure,*
> *whatever is lovely,*
> *whatever is of good repute,*
> *if there is any excellence*
> *and if anything worthy of praise,*
> *let your mind dwell on these things.*

C. S. Lewis put it in a nutshell when he said,

> *God cannot give us a happiness and peace apart from Himself, because it is not there. There is no such thing.*

Lewis was a brilliant man who did a lot of searching during his life. He eventually discovered that apart from God, there can be no happiness. Inside that nutshell was the kernel of truth that there must be faith in God's Word. Lewis put it as follows:

> *There are two kinds of people:*
> *those who say to God, "Thy will be done,"*
> *and those to whom God says,*
> *"All right, then, have it your way."*

People are generally miserable when left to their own devices, because they are always searching, but never coming to a knowledge of the truth.

May I always adhere to the advice in Philippians 4:4-8.

Soliloquy # 422

The Heavens Declare the Glory of God!

A friend
of my daughter took this picture
off the beach at Gulf Shores, AL

I was speechless....
The picture took my breath away!

Psalm 19:1 immediately invaded my thoughts!

*The heavens declare
the glory of God
and the earth
showeth forth His handiwork.*

How can my heart and mind
contain the beauty of God's creation?

How can I help but praise the Lord
for His great power and majesty?

Truly,
The heavens declare the Glory of God!

I thank the LORD!
And I praise His Holy Name!

Soliloquy #423

Under His Wings

Oh! My mind and heart are in jitters today.
Our lovely daughter is on the Gulf Coast,
and Hurricane Isaac is nearing landfall.
How I wish I were there with her!

Then I thought of many of our dear friends and neighbors in that area. My heart was very heavy, so I started praying for all of them. The God Who made the heavens and earth is still on the Throne!

As I was praying, the touching story of a mother hen invaded my senses. It is told that a raging fire was nearing her, threatening her and her chicks. How could she, a lowly mother hen, protect her little ones? She instinctively gathered her babies under her wings, protecting them the only way she knew how.

Later, firefighters found her charred body, burned to death. However when they moved her, they found all her little chicks, alive and safe. She had given her life for her chicks. This touching story brought to mind Scriptures that tell about being under God's wings:

Boaz acknowledged to Ruth (2:12)
that she had benefited from the LORD,
under whose wings
you have come to seek refuge.

The Psalmist also basked in the protection of the Lord.
Psalm 91:1 assures,
He who dwells in the shelter of the Most High
will abide in the shadow of the Almighty.

The Psalmist continued in verse 4,

*under **His** **wings** you may seek refuge;*
His faithfulness is a shield and bulwark.

I seem to feel the heartbreak of Jesus
when he saw the rebellion of the people of Jerusalem.
Matthew 23:37 recorded His graphic words:

O Jerusalem, Jerusalem,
who kills the prophets
and stones those who are sent to her!
*How often **I wanted to gather your children together,***
the way a hen gathers her chicks under her wings,
and you were unwilling.

The hymn writer, William O. Cushing (1823-1902)
wrote of God's protection,

Under His wings I am safely abiding;
Though the night deepens and tempests are wild,
Still I can trust Him, I know He will keep me;
He has redeemed me, and I am His child.
Under His wings, under His wings,
Who from His love can sever?
Under His wings my soul shall abide,
Safely abide forever.

There can be no safer place.
How often through life,
in the midst of all kinds of uncertainties and dangers,
I find great comfort in knowing that
He is keeping me
"under His wings."

Soliloquy # 424

God is Still on the Throne

My husband wrote: "First the Republican, and now the Democratic convention. In the past, there have been many political conventions, but I can't ever remember people being as nervous and concerned as they seem to be about the consequences of the next presidential election."

And so they should be. At least this is how I personally feel about conditions in the USA today. I think the words of Jesus in His Olivet Discourse (Luke 21:26) summarize how many people are disturbed: *Men's hearts failing them for fear, and for looking after those things which are coming on the earth.*

But God is still on the throne. I remember the words of Daniel concerning Nebuchadnessar (5:20): *...when his heart was lifted up and his spirit became so proud that he behaved arrogantly, he was deposed from his royal throne, and his glory was taken away from him.* I remember also the words in Daniel 11:22, *but the people who know their God will display strength and take action.*

A dear friend has reminded me any number of times, "It is more important to *know God*, than it is to know *about God*." There are also the words of Habakkuk 2:4. After exposing his concerns about conditions in Jerusalem and hearing what God was going to do about it, he reminded his readers that *The just shall live by his faith.*

And then he ended his prophecy by saying (Habakkuk 3:17-19): *Though the fig tree should not blossom, and there be no fruit on the vines, though the yield of the olive should fail, and the fields produce no food, though the flock should be cut off from the fold, and there be no cattle in the stalls, Yet I will exult in the LORD, I will rejoice in the God of my salvation. The Lord God is my strength, and He has made my feet like hinds' feet, and makes me walk on my high places.*

God is still on the throne. My husband reminded me of a chorus we used to sing many years ago. It goes, *God is still on the throne, and He will remember His own, Though trials may press us and burdens distress us He never will leave us alone. God is still on the throne, And he will remember his own. His promise is true, He will not forget you, God is still on the throne.*

Yes, God is still on the throne, but we must vote according to our Christian conscience. I have heard my husband quote the words of Oliver Cromwell many times: *"Trust in God, and keep your powder dry;" b*ecause all it takes for evil to succeed is for good men and women to do nothing.

Another passage of Scripture (Jeremiah 18:7-10) contains a warning from God:

*At one moment I might speak concerning a nation
or concerning a kingdom
to uproot, to pull down, or to destroy it;
If that nation against which I have spoken
turns from its evil.
I will relent concerning the calamity
I planned to bring on it.
Or at another moment,
I might speak concerning a nation
or concerning a kingdom
to build up or to plant it;
If it does evil in My sight by not obeying My voice,
then I will think better of the good
with which I had promised to bless it.*

Soliloquy #425

Learning from the Prophets

There are certain times when I think of something
I should have said to a particular person,
but the opportunity passes without me saying a thing.
There are other times when my heart pounds
making me conscious of something I should say,
but the time isn't right, or something seems to hold me back.

In recent days, I have been reading the Minor Prophets of the Old Testament. I marvel over the way the Lord seemed to put meaningful words into their mouths. They were "God's mouthpiece."

For example, Amos was a shepherd (vs. 1). Most likely he had no formal training at all. Yet the LORD called him to be a prophet to his people. The people were enjoying prosperity at the time. Often this caused people to forget God. Amos reminded them of the greatness of their God:

For behold, He who forms mountains
and creates the wind
and declares to man what are His thoughts,

He who makes dawn into darkness
And treads on the high places of the earth,

The LORD God of hosts is His name.
Amos 4:13

He who made the Pleiades and Orion
And changes deep darkness into morning,

Who also darkens day into night,

*Who calls for the waters of the sea
And pours them out on the surface of the earth,*

*The LORD is His name.
Amos 5:8 (NAS)*

Yes, God is all-powerful!
However, there were other prophets
who hesitated to do God's bidding.

Jonah was such an example. He went in the opposite direction to where God sent him. The result? He was caught in a mighty storm. He realized it was God intervening, so he told the sailors to throw him overboard. They did, but God prepared a great fish to swallow him.

Finally he realized the error of his ways and turned back to God, willing to obey His command. Then the LORD ordered the fish to vomit him out on the dry land. When God spoke again to Jonah, he obeyed and gave God's message.

May I learn from the prophets and obey the Lord's promptings.
I will pray with the Psalmist,

*Let the words of my mouth
and the meditations of my heart
be acceptable in Thy sight,
Oh Lord, my rock and my Redeemer.
Psalm 19:14*

Soliloquy # 426

Standing in the Need of Prayer

Not my brother, not my sister, but it's me O Lord,
standing in the need of prayer.
Not my father, not my mother, but it's me, O Lord,
standing in the need of prayer.
It's me, it's me, it's me O Lord;
standing in the need of prayer.

Yup, it's me who's standing in the need of prayer. Whenever I hear the daily news at home and abroad, I do not like to listen to it. Often lately, I find myself turning the TV off, or if that isn't possible, I go into another room. There's no doubt that these are troubling times.

It won't be long before Americans will be required to vote for a president of our country for the next four years. If I am honest, both of the men who wish to be president appear to be good, yet I feel uneasy about both of them. I Chronicles 12:22-23 asks the question, *"Where are the men who understand the times?"*

Appearing to be good is not enough. Yes,
Man looketh on the outward appearance,
but the Lord looketh on the heart. (1 Samuel 16:7)

Micah, one of the Minor Prophets of the Old Testament, spoke strongly against the leaders of his country. For it seemed they condoned immorality, social injustices, and the oppression of the poor. Did they really hate good and love evil as it seemed (3:2)? My heart breaks over the way so many people even today seem to be turning away from God. How long can evil go unpunished? There comes a time when judgment must fall. The prophet wrote,

Then they will cry out to the LORD,
but He will not answer them.
Instead, He will hide His face from them at that time,

> *because they have practiced evil deeds.*
> *Micah 3:4*

These are scary words. I thought of the wise man, Solomon, who penned the following proverbs,

> *My son, if you will receive my sayings,*
> *and treasure my commandments within you,*
> *Make your ear attentive to wisdom,*
> *Incline your heart to understanding;*
> *For if you cry for discernment,*
> *Lift your voice for understanding;*
> *If you seek her as silver, and search for her*
> *as for hidden treasures;*
> *Then you will discern the fear of the Lord,*
> *and discover the knowledge of God.*
> *For the LORD gives wisdom;*
> *from His mouth come knowledge and understanding.*
> *He stores up sound wisdom for the upright;*
> *He is a shield to those who walk in integrity,*
> *Guarding the paths of justice,*
> *and He preserves the way of His godly ones.*
> *Proverbs 2:1-8*

May I learn the experiential truths of these words, and may I earnestly seek the Lord to guide me in these difficult days!

> *Oh yes, it's me, it's me, it's me O Lord,*
> *standing in the need of prayer.*

Soliloquy #427

Filled With…What?

My computer is filled with something, but it isn't what I put there!

Instead it has been completely wiped out: my address book, all the emails I've sent, and all those that had been sent to me. Now, I cannot even get into it. So my daughter is letting me use her computer.

Someone has hacked into my account and sent out a distress call, as though it were from me. But it is one big lie. I'm told it said something to the effect that my family and I were in the United Kingdom and had been mugged and robbed. They claimed that we needed money.

Since all my addresses had been erased, I went to an old Juno account I'd had many years ago in order to let people know it was a scam.

I was feeling heartsick over the possibility that it might have caused anxiety among many of my friends, and worse yet, that some might have fallen for the scam and sent money.

However, in response to that email, many called or wrote back to the Juno address. Some caused many a chuckle and even a good laugh which helped to break the tension I was feeling.

One person wrote: "I cannot imagine you 'freaking out'" (as I had supposedly written, adding) "…everyone who knows you will recognize this immediately as a fraud!"

Another person wrote: "Shirley, I could tell by the grammar and non-reference to God that it wasn't you! I continue to enjoy your writings, please keep me on your list!"

Another wrote, "I knew it couldn't be you, because you'd be

asking for prayer, not for money!"

While my mind was in a state of agitation over this problem, I thought of references in the Bible warning about being filled with the wrong things.

For example, I thought of Ephesians 5:18:

> *Be not drunk with wine wherein is excess.*

Alcoholic beverage can take control, causing much anguish to others. Then that same verse continues:
> *but (keep being) filled with the Holy Spirit."*

I realize that whatever goes into my mind will come back to me, even sometimes waking me from sleep.

It brought back the verse I had quoted many times in Philippians 4:8 *(NAS)*. So the question: "Filled with…What?" It would be as the verse suggests:

> *…Whatever is true,*
> *whatever is honorable,*
> *whatever is right,*
> *whatever is pure,*
> *whatever is lovely,*
> *whatever is of good repute,*
> *if there is any excellence*
> *and if anything worthy of praise,*
> *let your mind dwell on these things."*

Soliloquy # 428

Travel & Reunions!

We've had some busy, but blessed days recently!

They began with our dear English friends who stopped for a few days visit. We were recalling that we have known each other for about sixty years.

How interesting is it that our time together, though always enjoyable and refreshing for both my husband and me, seems to have become sweeter as the years pass! We continue to thank the Lord for them and their friendship.

After they left, we began organizing and packing our car, because we had only the next day to get ready for winter in the south.

On the way south, we stopped in Ohio. What a great joy it was for us to be with our granddaughter and daughter! We were able to reunite with most of our extended family during the next week.

The day after we arrived in Ohio was another blessing, because we were able to renew fellowship with our family of saints at Calvary Chapel. Oh, the memories!

We recalled the home Bible studies nearly fifty years ago. Many of those same people had first come to know and love God's holy Word, and as a result they came to know Him personally.

We recalled how they felt the burden for their children. They wanted them to be able to hear the Word of God as they were doing. After many prayers went up unto God's throne of grace, the Lord led in astounding ways for the founding of Calvary Chapel.

Now after all these years, it is wonderful to renew our fellowship with those dear saints. Many of them were the original families that we had known 50 years ago. What memories we have!

This past Sunday, my husband spoke in Akron at a church founded by one of our own young people from Calvary Chapel. He began Bible Studies at a local golf course, and those studies grew until they felt led to begin a church. They were able to obtain beautiful facilities, complete with a small lake and a building where they are now meeting. It is always a joy to fellowship with them also.

Then immediately after the church service, our daughter drove us south to Alabama where we reside during the cold northern winters.

She has taken a week off work in order to, as she says, "renew her tan." We appreciated her doing most of the driving. We always enjoy spending uninterrupted time with her.

On arriving to our mobile home, tears were shed as we were joyfully reunited with our youngest daughter who lives next door to us.

Now we look forward to a time of renewal with our dear friends in the southern Alabama churches.

May the Lord continue to use us for His glory!

This is what the LORD says:
"Stop at the crossroads and look around
Ask for the old, godly way, and walk in it.
Jeremiah 6:16 (NLT)

Soliloquy # 429

Every Knee Shall Bow

During the night, the words from the Bible,
Hallowed be thy name came into my mind
and they wouldn't leave.

I started thinking,
'Yes, God's name should be honored,
for it is a name *above all names*.

He is King of kings and Lord of lords.

At His feet all nations will bow and confess that He is Lord.'

The words of Isaiah soon came into my mind,

For thus saith the LORD that created the heavens;
God Himself that formed the earth and made it;
He hath established it, he created it not in vain,
He formed it to be inhabited:
"I am the LORD, and there is none else....

...And there is no God else beside Me;
A just God and a Savior;
There is none beside Me.

Look unto Me, and be ye saved,
all the ends of the earth,
For I am God, and there is none else.
I have sworn by Myself,

The word has gone out of My mouth in righteousness,
And shall not return,

That unto Me every knee shall bow,
Every tongue will swear.
Isaiah 45:18, 21b-23 (KJV)

Philippians 2:10-11 repeats the prophecy:

That at the name of Jesus, every knee should bow…
And that every tongue should confess
that Jesus Christ is Lord,
To the glory of God the Father.

I get excited when I think of that day
when I will be able to fall on my knees before Him
and give Him all the praise, glory, and honor that is possible.
I will see Him "face to face."

But I wonder about the people
who have not bowed down to Him in this life.

The Bible says that every tongue will praise God,
every knee will swear allegiance that He is indeed God
--whether they want to admit it or not,
they will have to do it.

May they look to Him before it is too late.

Soliloquy # 430

Walking in the Light

"Walking"
It's just one word,
but the images that it brings to my mind are surprising!

I think of a little baby taking its first uncertain steps.
Then shortly afterward,
my mind switches to the thought of him
with his little hands in the air, waddling.
He is still uncertain, but he is gaining confidence.
Not long after that,
the image of a child running with his friends
replaces those previous pictures.

Soon more images appear:
a person speed walking along the side of the road;
then an athlete, striving to win a race.
But suddenly, the image of my poor husband
who is bent over because of the pain in his knee,
quickly replaces those previous images.
He is also striving…, walking…,
but he has to use the cane to steady himself.

Yes, walking conjures up many images.

God instructed Moses
as he was leading the Israelites through the wilderness:

Ye shall walk in all the way
which the LORD your God hath commanded you,
that ye may live,
and that it may be well with you,
and that ye may prolong your days
in the land which you shall possess

Deuteronomy 5:33.

But it is not only in the Old Testament
that there are these images of walking.
The apostle Paul also used the idea of walking when he said,
For we walk by faith, not by sight.
2 Corinthians 5:7

To make it even more clear, he told the Galatians:
this I say then, Walk in the Spirit,
and ye shall not fulfill the lust of the flesh.
Galatians 5:16

I remember attending the Lighthouse Fellowship Club.
It was a group of teen-aged Christian young people
from different churches in our area.
We met once a week, and at the beginning of each meeting,
we recited our key verse 1 John 1:7,

But if we walk in the light, as he is in the light,
We have fellowship one with another,
And the blood of Jesus Christ his Son
cleanseth us from all sin.

How many problems would be solved if Christians
could always walk with Jesus in His Light!

Soliloquy #431

Praises to the Most High

My heart was full of joy and praise
as I saw the dawn breaking this morning!

The birds outside seemed to be
whistling their praises to God.
The sun was shining brightly,
overtaking the mists and dusky dawn.
Soon everything was in radiant splendor.

Even though I already had my devotions,
I felt compelled to return to the Psalms
as I continued to bask in what I was seeing.

*It is good to give thanks to the LORD,
To sing praises to the Most High.*

*It is good to proclaim
your unfailing love
in the morning,
Your faithfulness in the evening.....*

*You thrill me, LORD, with all you have done for me.
I sing for joy because of what you have done.*

*O LORD, what great works you do!
And how deep are your thoughts.*

*Only a simpleton would not know,
And only a fool would not understand this:*

*Though the wicked sprout like weeds
And evildoers flourish, they will be destroyed forever.*

But you, O LORD, will be exalted forever.

*Your enemies, LORD, will surely perish;
All evildoers will be scattered....*

*But the godly will flourish like palm trees
and grow strong like the cedars of Lebanon.*

*For they are transplanted to the LORD's own house.
They flourish in the courts of our God.*

*Even in old age they will still produce fruit;
They will remain vital and green.*

*They will declare, 'The LORD is just!
He is my rock! There is no evil in him!'*

Psalm 92:1-2, 4-9, 12-15 (NLT)

Soliloquy # 432

Watch & Be Ready

My eyes can hardly believe the images
that have been on the television throughout this week.

Hurricane Sandy cast its destructive tentacles
over the Northern and Mid-Atlantic states,
reaching even inland with its wind and rain.

The storm surge ravished the land;
the strong winds and rain combined to take boats and ships
and cast them miles away from where they were moored;
multiple gas lines were broken,
spewing gas which erupted into fires
raging through neighborhoods.

As a result of these things,
almost everything in its path has been destroyed.

With good reason,
it has been called a "Monster Storm."

As my brain took in all those images,
I got a sick feeling in my stomach.

For even though many people heeded the warnings to evacuate
because of the size and strength of the coming storm,
many stayed.
They probably thought,
"Peace and safety."
Something like this had never happened to them before,
so the warnings went unheeded.

However, now they are left without power,
and darkness and destruction surround them.

Many have even been lost.

The images portrayed in the Bible
about the coming Day of the Lord
then flooded my mind,

*When people are saying,
'Everything is peaceful and secure,'*

*Then disaster will fall on them as suddenly
a pregnant woman's labor pains begin.
And there will be no escape.
1 Thessalonians 5:3 (NLT)*

The Bible warns of the aftermath of the coming disaster.
The important thing is to be ready.

*As it is appointed unto men once to die,
But after this the judgment;*

*So Christ was once offered
to bear the sins of many;*

*And unto them that look for him
shall he appear the second time
without sin unto salvation.
Hebrews 9:27-28 (KJV)*

Soliloquy 433

He is Still on the Throne!

Recently the soliloquy on my heart
was beating with a song
that we sang years ago with great gusto.
Now today, perhaps more timidly,
once again I find it remaining in my mind,

God is still on the throne
And He will remember His own;
Though trials may press us
And burdens distress us,
He never will leave us alone;

God is still on the throne
And He will remember His own;
His promise is true,
He will not forsake you,
Yes, God is still on the throne.

Regardless of how I feel
about the presidential election held this past week,
there are some Biblical principles that I must keep in mind.

Remember that I must be subject
to the governing authorities,
(Romans 13:1)

Remember that I am to obey God rather than man,
(Acts 5:29)

Remember that I must pray for those in authority,
(1 Tim. 2:1-2)

Remember that I am to live peaceably with all,

(Rom. 12:8)

Remember that my love should abound more and more,
(Phil. 1:9)

Remember that "all things work together for good
for those who love God," (Rom. 8:29)

Remember that "God is still on the throne,
(Psa. 45:6; 93:2)

Remember that God's word does not
return unto Him void. (Isa. 55:11)

Yes, God IS definitely still on the throne,
regardless of what some might think or even say.
So now, I am once again finding great comfort
in remembering what God has promised,

*…For He hath said,
I will never leave thee, nor forsake thee.
So that we may boldly say, The Lord is my helper,
and I will not fear what man shall do unto me.
Hebrews 13:5-6*

Soliloquy # 434

The Family of God

My Family!
What wonderful, warm feelings come with those two words!
They bring a smile to my face
and a sense of comfort to my inner being.
I feel fortunate to have belonged to a loving family
who sought to please the Lord.

Now that warm, wonderful feeling exists
for my own family:
My husband of 58 years
And my three grown children
Who have given me wonderful grandchildren
And even many very darling great-grandchildren.

Ah, yes, The Family!
Truly warm wonderful feelings
come to mind with every thought of each one of them.

The sense of belonging is very important to everyone.

However, there are some people who don't have
a close-knit family to which they feel they can belong.

As a result, they feel the need to look elsewhere.
They crave it!
Unfortunately, some of the places where they look for it,
they often find it being quite the opposite.

But there is good news for everyone.

And that good news is found in the Bible.

When Jesus was on earth,

he was told that his family
desired to speak with him.

He said,

*Who is my mother? And who are my brethren?
And he stretched forth his hand
toward his disciples, and said,
'Behold my mother and my brethren!*

*For whosoever shall do the will
of my Father which is in heaven,
The same is my brother, and sister, and mother.'
John 12:48-50*

How wonderful it is to know
that even those who do not belong
to an actual family here on earth
can still belong to the 'Family of God!'

I'm so glad I'm a part of the Family of God!
(Ephesians 3:14-15)

Soliloquy # 435

What Terrible Timing!

Some events of this past week and a half
were hard for me to understand,
And I thought, 'What terrible timing!'

My husband had a Total Knee Replacement.
His blood pressure dropped dangerously low
following the surgery,
so the doctors discontinued some of his medications.
In addition to that, his diabetes acted up
to the extent that his blood sugar soared.
As a result, he now is being given insulin shots.
I understand that after surgery, this sometimes happens.
Possibly it could be discontinued
when the intensity of his pain lowers.

During the afternoon,
I realized the battery of my cell phone was not holding a charge.
But my charger wasn't where it should have been in my purse.

I was staying at a friend's home
so I could be closer to the hospital.
When I got there, I looked in my overnight bag
and my computer bag,
but it was nowhere to be found!

At the same time, the cord to my computer failed to plug in,
so I wasn't able to keep in contact with anyone through it either.

I did feel cut off from everyone!
I thought, 'What terrible timing!
How unusual it is for my phone battery to be lost,
and also at the same time for my computer to be out of use!'

But then almost as soon as those thoughts entered my mind,

I thought, 'No, the Lord's timing is always perfect!
There must be a reason for all of this!'
I felt comforted, sensing His presence.

I awoke at 3:15 the next morning
and decided to slip out quietly
so I could drive back to our home
to look for it there.

Now, about a week later,
I'm grateful to a computer guy
who came and fixed my computer.
Of course, I found my phone plug also.
(I had put it in the side pocket of the car!)

After six days in the hospital,
my husband was transferred to a Rehabilitation Center
He is now receiving intense physical therapy there.
It is very painful for him.
But there are many friends of ours
who have had knee surgery.
They agree that it is not easy,
but it is certainly worth it!

So what helped me through those days
when I wondered about the 'terrible timing'?

*We know that all things work together
for good to them that love God,
to them who are the called
according to his purpose.
Romans 8:28*

Soliloquy # 436

Am I Ready?

I can't believe that it has been nearly three weeks
since my husband had his total knee replacement surgery.

That's probably because he has been staying
at the Health Care facility for physical therapy and rehabilitation
after his initial stay in the hospital.
So every day I've visited him during the days,
and then returned home to my duties afterwords.

But yesterday,
he started talking about coming home on Saturday!
And I realized that there are some things
that need to be changed before he is able to do so.

A handicapped bar needs to be installed in the bathroom,
and a ramp up the five steps to the porch would be helpful.
He will be able to go up the final step into our home
if another handicapped bar is installed outside the door.

It occurred to me that I had been drifting along during these days.
I knew that he would be coming home someday,
but when he said that he wanted to come home this weekend,
I realized that some changes needed to be made.

I was not ready!

So this morning as I was listing the things in my mind
that needed to be done before his return,
the chorus written by Fanny Crosby
came to me and I started to sing,

O can we say we are ready, brother?
Ready for the soul's bright home?

Say, will He find you and me still watching,
Waiting, waiting when the Lord shall come?

I need to ask myself,
am I ready for His return
or must there be changes made?
The Bible says,

Be ready always to give an answer
to every man that asketh you
a reason of the hope that is in you
with meekness and fear....

Feed the flock of God which is among you,...
Willingly,...of a ready mind,....
being ensamples to the flock.

And when the chief Shepherd shall appear,
Ye shall receive a crown of glory
that fadeth not away.
1 Peter 5:2-4

Yes, I must have a ready mind,
and I must be an example to others.
The apostle Paul said that he was

ready to preach the gospel
and
to be ready for every good work
Romans 1:15; Titus 3:1

Soliloquy # 437

"If That Isn't Love"

Love! What is love anyway?

It's nice having my husband home again.
Whenever he asks me to get his shoes,
or get some ice for his knee,
I am so used to doing what he asks,
that I do it.

Besides, I feel sorry for him
because of the pain
he is still having.
I don't like to see him suffer.

But the other day when my daughter was here,
she immediately said,
"Mom! If you loved him,
you'd let him get it himself!
He needs to walk and get exercise! "

As I was thinking of her words this morning,
I mused, 'What is Love?'
Probably a large part of it would be to desire
and do what is best for the recipient of my love.

But how can I do that when it causes him pain?

But I suppose that is what God did when
He sent His only begotten Son into the world
so that those who believe in Him
could have everlasting life (John 3:16).
That had to be hard!

Then to see Him suffer some 30 years later,

and to even forsake Him
because of the sin of the world
that He took on Himself (2 Corinthians 5:21).
That had to be really hard!

The haunting song comes to my mind,
I believe it was written by Dottie Rambo,

He left the splendor of heaven
Knowing His destiny was the lonely hill of Golgotha
There to lay down His life for me

And if that isn't love
Then the ocean is dry, there's no stars in the sky
And the sparrows can't fly
Yeah if that isn't love then heaven's a myth
There's no feeling like this if that isn't love.

Yes, that is Amazing Love,
such love that it is difficult to comprehend!

Thanks be unto God
for His unspeakable gift.
2 Corinthians 9:15

So I need to remember God's amazing gift,
and let that be an example of true love for me!

Soliloquy # 438

Little Baby No Longer!

What a darling little baby boy I saw recently!
He was wrapped in a soft blue lightweight blanket
and must have been no more than a few weeks old.
My heart had a strong yearning to hold him.
I thought of how long ago it has been
since I held my own children.
I also remembered how much I enjoyed
holding my grandchildren and watching them grow!
Now I have great-grandchildren,
however the time I get to spend with them
seems to be so much less.

Then probably because it is the Christmas season,
my thoughts drifted to Mary, the mother of Jesus.
I pondered,
'How could her mind have comprehended
the magnitude of the fact that she was holding in her arms
God manifested in the flesh?'
Angels even announced his arrival to the shepherds.
As I lingered on these thoughts,
I realized the impossibility
of leaving that little baby in a manger.
It was definitely an amazing event.
The Bible continues (Luke 2:52),

And Jesus increased in wisdom and stature,
And in favour with God and man.

He grew and continued to be a perfect example for mankind.
Even in adulthood He did not stray from the purpose

for which He was sent by God into the world (John 3:16). He had primarily one goal, and that was to do the will of the One Who had sent Him. He said in John 4:34,

*My meat is to do the will of him that sent me,
And to finish his work.*

What was that "work?" It was as 2 Corinthians 5:21 states,

*For he hath made him to be sin for us,
who knew no sin;
That we might be made
the righteousness of God in him.*

Just as He must not be left in the cradle, neither should He be left on the cross. For the Bible continues to point to the glorious climax found in Revelation 11:15,

*For the kingdoms of this world
are become the kingdoms of our Lord, and of his Christ;
And he shall reign forever and ever.*

Soliloquy # 439

Through It All

Oh my!
How is it possible that it is almost a new year once again?
It seems like yesterday that there was anxiety
with the thought of turning the calendar from 1999 to 2000.
Yet now, here it is so many years later,
and we are ready to begin another new calendar year.

Looking back over this past year,
I thought of the various changes,
such as how the shorelines seemed to have changed
due to the magnitude of hurricanes.

Tornadoes also wrecked havoc,
leaving people homeless,
trying to salvage and rebuild.

Some very dear friends left this life
to realize the blessedness of being with the Lord.
I find comfort in the knowledge
that though they are absent from the body,
they are present with the Lord,
and I will be seeing them again one day!
(1 Cor. 5:8; 1 Thess. 4:13-18)

Also there are many who are suffering pain and afflictions.
Yes, while on this earth, there is suffering.
Jesus said,

...In the world you have tribulation,

*But take courage,
I have overcome the world.
John 15:33*

Years ago, my husband and I heard Dallas Holmes singing.
This past week, one of the songs he sang
has been running through my mind
as I have been contemplating this past year,

*I've been to lots of places, and I've seen a lot of faces.
There've been times I felt so all alone.
But in my lonely hours, yes, those precious lonely hours,
Jesus let me know that I was His own.
I thank God for the mountains, and I thank Him for the valleys.
I thank Him for the storms He brought me through,
For if I'd never had a problem
I wouldn't know that He could solve them,
I'd never know what faith in God could do.
Through it all, through it all,
I've learned to trust in Jesus,
I've learned to trust in God.
Through it all, through it all,
I've learned to depend upon His Word."*

How I thank the Lord
for His continued presence and encouragement
through all circumstances
all throughout the past year!

Soliloquy # 440

The Light's Out!

About a month ago, my daughter came over with anticipation!
She proudly gave me a series of tall, thin buildings.

There was a post office, a hotel,
a grocery store, a toy/gift store, and a church.
Small Christmas tree bulbs illuminated the insides of them,
causing all the windows to light up.
It looked so cheery!

I immediately put them on our tall counter.
All through the month we thoroughly enjoyed seeing them
when she came over for a cappuccino each morning!

But one morning,
the light of the church building was out!
As I thought about it later,
I began to wonder:

'Oh dear,' I thought,
'I hope this isn't indicative
of what's happening
in some of our churches today.'

I had just finished reading the book of the Revelation,
and felt saddened by the words of Jesus to the church at Ephesus.
He began by praising all their good works
for they were doing everything right!
But then, he went on,

*Nevertheless I have somewhat against thee,
because thou hast left thy first love.
Revelation 2:4*

I had to remember that whenever the Bible refers to the church,
it isn't referring to a building, but to the people who are inside.
It seems as if so many people go through the motions
when they are in church and maybe even when they are outside.
They seems like they are Christians,
but inside their innermost beings,
hey are far from the Lord.

When Jesus was on earth,
He quoted Isaiah using words about their religious leaders,

*This people draweth nigh unto me with their mouth,
and honoureth me with the lips;
but their heart is far from me.
Matthew 15:8 from Isaiah 29:13*

Even though it might be possible,
I pray that it might never be true of me.
May the light and love of Jesus
always shine through me.

Soliloquy # 441

Pain?

Pain is all around me.
My husband's knee,
my daughter's toe,
my granddaughter's nausea,
and the list goes on and on.
Few people are without pain.

The Bible has much to say about it.
For example,

David, the psalmist, anguished,

*Turn thee unto me,
and have mercy upon me;
for I am desolate and afflicted.
The troubles of my heart are enlarged:
O bring thou me out of my distresses.
Look upon mine affliction and my pain;
and forgive all my sins.
Psalm 25:16-18*

Jesus gave great comfort when He said,

*These things I have spoken unto you
that in me ye might have peace.
In the world ye shall have tribulation:
but be of good cheer;
I have overcome the world.
John 16:33*

Peter told the crowd at Pentecost that had gathered
that Jesus loosed the pains of death! (Acts 2:22-24).

The apostle Paul knew pain from experience. He wrote:

*For we know that the whole creation groaneth
and travaileth in pain together until now.
Romans 8:28*

The apostle John, writing about the new heaven and the new earth
that will someday come down from heaven, said he heard
a great voice out of heaven saying (Revelation 21:3-4),

*Behold, the tabernacle of God is with men,
and he will dwell with them, and they shall be his people,
and God himself shall be with them, and be their God.
And God shall wipe away all tears from their eyes;
and there shall be no more death,
neither sorrow, nor crying,
neither shall there be any more pain:
for the former things are passed away.*

How wonderful it is to be assured
that all this pain and suffering will someday be abolished!
The sufferings of this present are not worthy to be compared
with the glory that will be revealed in us (Romans 8:18).

Soliloquy #442

Psalm 139

This Psalm has been very special to my husband and me while he was in the hospital:

*O LORD, you have examined my heart
and know everything about me.
You know when I sit down or stand up.
You know my thoughts even when I'm far away.
You see me when I travel and when I rest at home.
You know everything I do.
You know what I am going to say
even before I say it, LORD.
You go before me and follow me.
You place your hand of blessing on my head.
Such knowledge is too wonderful for me,
too great for me to understand!*

*I can never escape from your Spirit!
I can never get away from your presence!
If I go up to heaven, you are there;
If I go down to the grave, you are there.
If I ride the wings of the morning,
If I dwell by the farthest oceans,
even there your hand will guide me,
and your strength will support me.
I could ask the darkness to hide me
and the light around me to become night--
but even in darkness I cannot hide from you.
To you the night shines as bright as day,
Darkness and light are the same to you.*

*You made all the delicate, inner parts of my body
and knit me together in my mother's womb.
Thank you for making me so wonderfully complex!
Your workmanship is marvelous--
how well I know it.
You watched me as I was being formed in utter seclusion,
as I was woven together in the dark of the womb.
You saw me before I was born.
Every day of my life was recorded in your book.
Every moment was laid out
before a single day had passed.*

*How precious are your thoughts about me, O God.
They cannot be numbered! I can't even count them;
they outnumber the grains of sand!
And when I wake up, you are still with me!*

*O God, if only you would destroy the wicked!
Get out of my life, you murderers!
They blaspheme you, your enemies misuse your name.
O LORD, shouldn't I hate those who hate you?
Shouldn't I despise those who oppose you?
Yes, I hate them with total hatred,
for your enemies are my enemies.*

*Search me, O God, and know my heart;
test me and know my anxious thoughts.
Point out anything in me that offends you,
and lead me along the path of everlasting life.*

Soliloquy # 443

I Can Imagine!

His mother wrote me an email today
telling me that the Lord took her beloved son
"home this morning to be singing with his Daddy and cousin."

I imagined the scene occurring in heaven.
I saw multitudes of people of every nation,
some who possibly previously hadn't even had pleasing voices.

They joined them making beautiful harmonies.
They all now are pain-free and disease-free.
And they have perfect voices,
all praising our wonderful Lord and Savior,
Who died for them and rose again!

Then I thought of the grand welcoming of all those
whose lives had been touched by this new arrival.
Some knew him as a boy,
some knew him as a newly married man
whose life had turned upside down
by the devastating news of cancer
that was predicted to soon take his body.
Some knew him as a living miracle
of God's wondrous healing hand time after time.
Some knew him as a comforter standing by their side
while they underwent life's challenges.
Some knew him as a witness to them,
sharing God's love and matchless grace
showing the way to their eternal home.
Some knew him as a godly pastor and friend.

And then he saw JESUS!
He was the epitome of true joy and peace
as he beheld Him face to face in all of His glory!

Pastor Greg, we have loved you dearly,
and will miss you immensely.
Your influence will continue here on earth
because of the tremendous testimony
you've had in so many lives.

We are happy for you, but will miss you.
We cling to the comfort and promises
found in 1 Thessalonians 4, and 1 Corinthians 15.

The Bible says:

*Precious in the sight of the LORD
is the death of his saints.
Psalm 116:15*

Soliloquy # 444

Jesus: A Friend Indeed!

"Oh my! Sometimes life does seem to be overwhelming!"

I suppose it must have been building up over the last three months
since my husband began his hospital visits,
surgeries, and rehab, but I didn't realize it.

I had fallen in the middle of the night rushing to the hospital.
So a friend recommended that I go to her chiropractor.
I had been under the impression that my insurance would cover it.
However, after I had already gone multiple times,
I discovered that it wasn't covered.
That fact hit me like a ton of bricks,
and I suddenly seemed to be overwhelmed!

But my dear husband was nearby when I received that call,
and he said, "Don't worry about it. We'll just pay bit by bit.
It'll be OK. The treatment has been good for you."

Interestingly, I had been reading a book by Rebecca Carey Lyles,
(*Winds of Wyoming),* and had written down a quote from it.
It went as follows:

*The only friend in high places that counts is God.
Even though he's above and beyond all,
he's a friend who sticks closer than a brother,
because he lives within us.
He's a friend who walks before us,
beside us and behind us,
a friend who promised to never leave us
or turn his back on us."*

I remembered how Moses told Joshua
that the LORD was with him (Deut.31:6,8),

He it is that doth go with thee...
He it is that doth go before thee;
He will be with thee,
He will not fail thee,
neither forsake thee.
It is repeated in Hebrews 13:5-6:
"I will never leave thee nor forsake thee.

Suddenly, as if to make an indelible imprint on my mind,
I thought of another friend who asked me to play something
on my little harp about the wonderful, matchless name of Jesus.

'Yes!' I thought, 'Get your mind back on Jesus!
What a friend He's been through all of this!'

Have we trials and temptations?
Is there trouble anywhere?
We should never be discouraged,
Take it to the Lord in prayer..
Can we find a friend so faithful
Who will all our sorrows share?
Jesus knows our eve'ry weakness,
Take it to the Lord in prayer.
   — Joseph Scriven, 1820-1886

It's true -- I can still count on my dearest Friend
to be there for me at all times! Philippians 4:13,19:

I can do all things through Christ
Who strengthens me...
My God shall supply all your need
...by Christ Jesus!

Soliloquy # 445

My Wandering Mind

My mind has really been wandering today....

I was sitting on my Lazy Boy rocker with the door closed.
I didn't want to disturb my husband who was talking a nap.
My fingers were caressing my little baby blue harp,
soothing my soul. I was playing
What A Friends We Have in Jesus.

But immediately, I began to play the beautiful song,

I come to the garden alone
while the dew is still on the roses.
And the voice I hear sounding in my ear
The Son of God discloses.
And He walks with me, and He talks with me.
And He tells me I am his own.
And the joy we share as we tarry there
None other has ever known.

I thought of the phone call that I had received earlier....
The daughter of a dear friend in Florida
left a message that her mother had passed away,
and was now in heaven with Jesus.

So as I was playing my harp and meditating,
I thought of her being in the garden with Jesus
and I imagined her now playing a harp also!

I smiled as I remembered whenever I visited her,
we would play her instruments together....

She had an organ and a piano, we played them together....
She had a couple accordions and we played them together.

Sometimes I'd play my little harp with her on the organ.
It was always such a joy being with her!
She was an amazing lady.

Strangely my mind drifted to something I had witnessed recently.
My husband and I were sitting on a bench at the beach
enjoying the sunshine and solitude there when
I noticed about a dozen seagulls standing in a row on the shore,
all looking out over the water.
It seemed very unusual to me.

As I thought of my friend's recent death,
and the words of the songs I had been playing,
the sight of these gulls sitting all in a row
all looking out over the Gulf,
sent my mind to what might be a scene in heaven.

I imagined those gulls watching my friend playing an instrument
with many other dear friends and relatives nearby.
They were all worshiping the Lord,
singing his praises together.
It made a joyous scene!

It reminded me of multitudes recorded in the book of Revelation,
who with loud voices were praising the LORD:

*Worthy is the Lamb that was slain
to receive power, and riches,
and wisdom, and strength, and honour,
and glory, and blessing...
Revelation 5:12*

Then I had to begin praising the Lord also!

Soliloquy # 446

All That I Really Need

I could see, feel, and hear the words
written in the New Living Translation of Psalms 34:5-11.

As I meditated on them, my heart was touched...

Your unfailing love, O LORD,
is as vast as the heavens;
your faithfulness reaches beyond the clouds.

Oh my! When I see the vastness of the night's sky
with its millions of stars, it renders me speechless.
There would be no way to measure the faithfulness of the Lord,
for He always remains faithful!

Your righteousness is like the mighty mountains,
Your justice like the ocean depth.

How could one measure the righteousness
or the justice of the Lord?
It would be impossible.

You care for people and animals alike, O LORD
How precious is your unfailing love, O God!

Yes, God's love and care comfort me at all times – there's no
disappointment in the LORD!

All humanity finds shelter in the shadow of your wings.
You feed them from the abundance of your own house,
letting them drink from your river of delights.
For you are the fountain of life,
the light by which we see.

I am safe in the shadow of His wings.
He supplies my every need.

*Pour out your unfailing love on those who love you.
Give justice to those with honest hearts.*

The songwriter, John C. Hallett, in 1940 wrote:

*All that I need is in Jesus,
He's all that He promised to be.
His love and His care comfort me everywhere.
There is no disappointment in Him.*

Just as this beautiful world that He created
satisfies my every yearning for beauty;
God's love, care, and faithfulness
is ready to supply my every emotional need.

Yes, all that I need is in the LORD, my God!

Soliloquy # 447

Casting Care Where?

Casting all your care upon Him;
for He careth for you.
1 Peter 5:7

How often has this verse come to mind over the years?
Times without number!

Looking back,
I can remember reciting it from memory
when I was a child.

My older sister kept encouraging me
to memorize verses from the Bible,
and I dutifully did what she asked. How I thank her!
Once I had memorized one verse,
she always had another.

However, while I was reading the book of Mark the past few days,
1 Peter 5:7 seemed to plant itself deeper in my heart.

In scene after scene, Mark recorded how
Jesus saw needs and filled them.

Mark 1:23, Jesus saw a man with an unclean spirit,
so He commanded that spirit to come out of him.
Mark 1:27 states that people were amazed over His great authority,
that even the unclean spirits obeyed Him.
Indeed, His fame spread throughout all the region of Galilee.
And so it continued...
verses 29-34 tell about Him healing Simon's wife.
Then in the evening,
He healed many more and cast out many devils

Whenever and wherever He happened to be,

if He saw someone in need, He stopped and met that need.

Suddenly as I was reading the 9th chapter of Mark,
1 Peter 5:7 took on a more significant meaning to me.
I realized again that Peter was not just stating
an ambiguous promise.
I can bank on it,
because Jesus proved Who He was
and what His desires were
even while He was on earth.

No matter what He was doing or where He was going,
He continued to meet the needs of people.
And He does so even today.

For example, I was getting quite nervous
before playing a solo on my harp at church,
but then I remembered Philippians 4:19, 13:

My God shall supply all your need....
I can do all things through Christ
Who strengthens me.

So I cast my cares on the Lord,
reminding Him that He promised to supply all my needs,
praying that He would use my little harp for His glory.

Soliloquy # 448

Gird up the Mind?

Gird up the loins of your mind....
1 Peter 1:13

So what does this mean...*gird up the loins of my mind?*

It somehow brought the image of the girdles that women
used to wear in the early years of the 1900's.
They had ties something like shoelaces through
quite a stiff garment around the mid-section of their bodies.
They would have to pull the laces tightly
to squeeze themselves into an hourglass figure.
No loose flab flopping around anywhere.

I also thought of how my mind would wander,
especially during those early morning Bible readings,
or even at times while listening to a message.
Then I have to pray that the Lord would
pull my thoughts together
or *'gird' up my mind"*

I decided to check another translation to possibly get more insights
The New Living Bible's translators penned the words:

So think clearly and exercise self-control.

That does help me.
I need to consciously exercise control over my mind
so that I can think clearly and understand
what the Lord is telling me.
Understanding is important.

Interestingly, the apostle Peter
continued his exhortations by saying:

*Look forward to the gracious salvation
that will come to you
when Jesus Christ is revealed to the world.*

*So you must live as God's obedient children.
Don't slip back into your old ways of living
to satisfy your own desires.*

*You didn't know any better then.
But now you must be holy in everything you do,
just as God who chose you is holy.
1 Peter 1:13-15*

Oh yes! I must think clearly and rejoice in the fact
that when Jesus returns the second time,
it will be salvation from this world
and its increasingly sinful ways;
salvation for my body
that seems to daily continue to lose its vitality;
and salvation from the wrath of God
which is the penalty of sin
(Romans 5:9; 1 Thessalonians 5:9).

AND I'll enter into the full realization of eternal life
with my Lord and Savior, Jesus Christ!
(Titus 1:2; 3:7).

Soliloquy # 449

What's on My Mind?

What's on your mind?
'Nothin' much,' is often the common answer.

So I started thinking about a person's mind.
Surprisingly, all kinds of quips surfaced:

'A person uses a very small portion of the mind.'
'The mind is like a muscle in the way that it can be expanded.'
"One can never learn too much.'
'Your mind just keeps growing....'
'You don't use it, you lose it!'

It is astounding to think of all that is stored
in the recesses of the mind!
However, it seems the older I get,
the longer it seems for me to recall something.

I remember a social scientist who likened the mind to a computer.
When the computer is new, things can be retrieved in a flash.
But as the computer gets older
and more is stored in it,
the slower it becomes.

As I continued to think about a person's mind,
verses in the Bible kept surfacing.
The second chapter of Philippians kept coming to mind.
And it seemed to speak to me:

Let this mind be in you, which was also in Christ Jesus:
Who being in the form of God,
thought it not robbery to be equal with God:

But made himself of no reputation,
and took upon him the form of a servant,

and was made in the likeness of men:
and being found in fashion as a man,
he humbled himself,
and became obedient unto death,
even the death of the cross.

This was the heart of this great gospel of salvation.

The apostle Peter wrote that the prophets prophesied
and wanted to know more about it.
He told them about Christ's suffering
and His coming great glory.
He said that even the angels were watching
and wondering when these things would happen.

But he didn't stop there,
he told them that it wasn't only
for those to whom he was writing,
but for others also!
(1 Peter 1:10-13)

His culminating charge was,

Therefore, gird your minds for action.
1 Peter 1:13

This is good advice.
I must focus my mind
on these things concerning the gospel..
And then, I must be prepared to take action
and share it with others.

Soliloquy# 450

Resting Where?

Last night I was extremely tired!
So I decided to go to bed and read for a while.
Some time later, I turned out the light, but I couldn't seem to relax.

I rested a bit, it's true, but restlessness was gaining ground.
All kinds of thoughts were running through my mind!
Strange ones!
After I wondered about them for a while,
I decided I'd better give them to the Lord.

Still I couldn't get to sleep.
So I began to meditate on my Lord and Savior.
His Word began to enter my restless mind
and calmed my spirit.
I felt a smile come to my face
and peace replaced the restlessness.
Soon I fell asleep.

Interestingly,
part of my Bible reading this morning was Psalm 63.
I marveled over the way the Lord's hand
is so often evident in my life,
and I praised and thanked Him for it.

*I lie awake thinking of you,
meditating on you through the night.*

The Psalmist seemed to have experienced
some of the same things that I had.

*Because you are my helper,
I sing for joy in the shadow of your wings.*

This verse reminded me of yesterday afternoon.

I had relaxed outside,
and the birds were sweetly singing their songs.

After enjoying their fascinating melodies,
I envisioned them praising the Lord.

I thought of the image of a mother bird sitting on her nest,
contentedly protecting her little peeps under her wings.

The Psalmist continued,

*I cling to you;
your strong right hand holds me securely.
Psalm 63:6-8 (NLT)*

How wonderful it is to know that the Lord is my helper,
that He protects me, and that He holds me securely.

So all I have to do
is to be *resting* completely *in Him*,
being consciously aware that He is the One
Who protects and calms my restless spirit.

Soliloquy 451

At the Top

Imagine what it would feel like
to be at the top of everything you ever desired in life
— of having reached life's most desired goal.

It might be a desire to have climbed Mt Everest,
or to have won a gold medal at the Olympics.
It might be a desire to have been at the head of a huge corporation,
or to have gained a top award in the Music or Film Industry.
It might even have been the winner in a Dog Show,
or of the envied Grand Prix.

What must it feel like to be at the top?
The winner makes a name for him or her self,
and quite often sees his or her name in the headlines.

These thoughts came to mind recently when my daughter shared
pictures that her son (my grandson) had sent her.

He had the opportunity to take photos for an Indy car team
at the Honda Grand Prix in St. Petersburg recently.
What an experience that would have been
to have been so close to those cars going 140+ miles per hour.
He said it changed everything he ever understood about speed!

I thought to myself,
'How exciting it would be for those people to be at the top.
However, that could easily change within a short time.'

Interestingly, the Bible tells of Someone
who was at the very top place imaginable.
Yet He gave it all up!
It is recorded in the book to the Philippians.

...Christ Jesus,
Who, being in the form of God,
thought it not robbery to be equal with God:
But made himself of no reputation,
and took upon him the form of a servant,
and was made in the likeness of men:
And being found in fashion as a man,
he humbled himself,
and became obedient unto death,
even the death of the cross.

That seemed as if it were a GREAT fall!
From the highest position possible,
to the lowest of the low.
But the Bible doesn't stop there!
It continues telling of a great day in the future:

Wherefore God also hath highly exalted him
and given him a name which is above every name:
That at the name of Jesus every knee should bow
And that every tongue should confess
that Jesus Christ is Lord,
to the glory of God the Father.
Philippians 2:5-11

May these facts take a greater personal hold of my life.

Soliloquy 452

Coming Soon!

My Grandson is coming for a visit soon!
Needless to say, my daughter can hardly contain herself,
she is so excited!

She's been preparing for his coming for days now:
She's been doing extra cleaning around her house --
actually hauling furniture outside to thoroughly clean them.
Since he's a great photographer,
she's been planning special places where they can go
so that he will be able to get some good pictures.

As I've been thinking about her eagerness
over this wonderful occasion,
it occurred to me how similar this should be
to the Christian's anticipation
of the coming of the Lord Jesus Christ.

But alas, how often it seems that life
simply goes on from day to day.
No, the house doesn't get put in order;
often neither does a person's life change
as a result of the knowledge of His return.

While Jesus was on earth,
He warned people about His second coming.
He gave some examples, such as in the days of Noah,
they were eating and drinking,
going about their daily activities,
not believing Noah's warning.
But the great flood did come,
and unfortunately for them,
then it was too late.

My daughter is fortunate in that she knows
exactly when her son is scheduled to arrive.
So she is preparing for his visit!

However, we do not know exactly
when the Lord Jesus Christ will return.
But we are assured that He will come again.
As He was ascending into the clouds,
the people saw and heard two men in white apparel say:

*...this same Jesus,
which is taken up from you into heaven,
shall so come in like manner
as ye have seen him go into heaven.
Acts 1:11*

Matthew, chapters 24 and 25, record
how Jesus told other examples of people who weren't ready,
who were careless in their responsibilities.
They suffered because of it.

He told the people:

*Watch therefore,
for ye know neither the day nor the hour
wherein the Son of man cometh.
Matthew 25:13*

My daughter is ready for her son's coming --
Now I need to be sure
that I am ready for God's Son's coming.

Soliloquy 453

Soaking It All Up

It felt wonderful to be soaking it all up!

My daughter flew in from Ohio to drive us back north.
She planned several days off work
so we could have time to go to the beach
and soak up some of the sun's rays before we left.

Oh, how relaxing it was to spread out a sheet
on that beautiful beach and relax,
listening to the waves gently rolling up on the shore.
Soon she walked along the beach with her feet in the water.

Feeling the soothing sun on our sun-deprived skin
seemed to melt all the cares of the winter away.
Most of my winter had seemed to be involved with
taking my husband to hospitals, rehabilitation facilities,
physical therapy, and doctor's offices.

When my daughter arrived, her generous nature
anticipated needs and immediately filled them.

For example, our porch and ramp needed work.
It was a job that my husband and I
could not have handled by ourselves.
She encouraged me to go with her to pick out a stain.
She got the things we needed and we began...
My husband came out and was able to stand
so he could paint some of the outside spindles,
while she and I worked on the inside of them.
Finally she finished the floor and ramp by herself.
Later in the day, we stood back, a bit stain-speckled,
but feeling very pleased with the finished product!

As I looked at the deck,
I remembered how that dry wood
seemed to soak up the stain.
It seemed to be anticipating the application.
It literally ate it up, absorbing it very quickly!

Then I thought of the expressions on some people's faces
when my husband preached.
They seemed to be starved for the Word of God,
and so they eagerly seemed to soak in every word.

The Bible says,

*So shall my word be
that goeth forth out of my mouth:
it shall not return unto me void.
Isaiah 55:11*

God's Word is not just pretty platitudes,
it actually answers the questions to man's needs.

*Blessed are they which do
hunger and thirst after righteousness,
for they shall be filled.
Matthew 5:6*

It's true that my whole being anticipates the time
that I set aside in order to soak up God's Word!

Soliloquy # 454

The Example of God's Love

My husband was mentioning the church in Ephesus
how they had lost their first love.
They didn't love God or others the way they did at first.
According to Revelation, chapter 2,
God was going to remove their witness.

Later, as I was meditating on these things,
I thought how sometimes this does actually happen.
If a group doesn't show genuine concern and love for others,
soon people will leave.
Most people do not want to stay
where they feel that they are not wanted.
And as people leave,
the witness dies.

This should never happen in a church family!
It is important to show love for one another.

Jesus said,

A new commandment I give unto you:
That ye love one another as I have loved you,
that ye also love one another.
By this shall all men know that ye are my disciples
in that ye have love for one another.
John 13:34-35 (KJV)

However, the Bible carries it a step further.
According to 2 Corinthians 5:14,

The love of Christ constrains us.

I wonder if this could mean that
even though 'love' isn't first received,
it should still be given?

I remember reading the little quip:

"First I learned to love my teacher.
Then I learned to love my teacher's Bible.
Finally I learned to love my teacher's God!

What was it about my teacher that I learned to love?
Perhaps it was that I felt
that she was genuinely concerned and cared for me.
Naturally it followed that I wanted to listen to her.
And then I learned to love what she loved.
She became my example.

I saw her showing great interest in her Bible.
When I realized that the Bible was telling about God
and His great love for me,
I wanted to love Him also.

1 John 4:19 states:

*We love Him,
because He first loved us.*

He set a great example for me to follow!

Soliloquy # 455

Peaceful Relaxing Rest

Photograph taken by my grandson,
Matthew Lower,
at Bellengrath Gardens, Mobile Alabama

He leadeth me beside the still waters....

Psalm 23:2

As soon as my eye beheld this scene,

my whole being seemed to relax.

God's love and faithfulness surrounded me

as I absorbed the beauties of His creation.

Then I thought of His unfailing love and leading!

It is good to give thanks to the Lord,

to sing praises to the Most High.

It is good to proclaim

your unfailing love in the morning,

your faithfulness in the evening.

Psalm 92:1-2 (NLT)

Soliloquy # 456

Bless the LORD

The words of Psalm 103 grabbed my heart this morning,
and I had to praise and pray along with the Psalmist:

Bless the LORD, O my soul:
and all that is within me,
bless his holy name.
Bless the LORD, O my soul,
and forget not all his benefits:

And there have been so many – too numerous to count;
so I continued to repeat the words of the Psalmist:

For as the heaven is high above the earth,
so great is his mercy toward them that fear him.
As far as the east is from the west,
so far hath he removed our transgressions from us.

Like as a father pitieth his children,
so the LORD pitieth them that fear him.
For he knoweth our frame;
he remembereth that we are dust.

As for man, his days are as grass;
as a flower of the field, so he flourisheth.
For the wind passeth over it, and it is gone;
and the place thereof shall know it no more.

What a contrast human frailties are
with the love and mercy of the LORD!

*But the mercy of the LORD
is from everlasting to everlasting
upon them that fear him,
and his righteousness
unto children's children;
To such as keep his covenant
and to those that remember
his commandments
to do them.*

*Bless the LORD,
all his works
in all places of his dominion:
bless the LORD, O my soul.*

Psalm 103:1-2; 11-18; 22 (KJV)

Oh yes, with my whole heart,
I will bless the LORD!

May I never forget
the good things
He does for me.

Soliloquy # 457

One Step at a Time

After a person completes one step successfully,
it is possible to go on to the next.

So it was at my local church this past Sunday.
My pastor presided over the final phase of a building program
that was begun ten years ago.

Phase one, or the first step, began
with the expansion of the worship sanctuary
and additional space.

Some time after that, Phase two was started,
and the congregation cooperated again
by approving that phase of the expansions.

Finally Phase three was presented
and received congregational approval.
With anticipation, the "ground-breaking" occurred
for the completion of the long-term building program.

At one time it all seemed to be so far in the distant future.
What a joyous occasion it was to finally see this dream!

It occurred to me how this is like a person's development.
A babe's early months can only handle milk.
As the baby grows, gradually the mother
adds some solid foods, making sure the
baby's system can handle it.
As each step in this process is successful,
the child is introduced to other foods,
eventually becoming a healthy,
mature individual,
able to eat anything.

So it is with the Christian life.
When a person accepts the Lord Jesus Christ as personal Savior,
that person is a "babe in Christ,"
and must be fed and treated as a babe.

As newborn babes,
desire the sincere milk of the word,
that ye may grow thereby.
1 Peter 2:2

As one grows and develops gradually,
more "foods" and "life experiences" are presented.
As each step is completed successfully,
a further experience is received,
so that eventually the babe-in-Christ
becomes a fully matured person in Christ.

God's Word does give a word of caution about stunted growth,

For when for the time ye ought to be teachers,
ye have need that one teach you again
which be the first principles of the oracles of God;
and are become such as have need of milk,
and not of strong meat.
For every one that useth milk
is unskilful in the word of righteousness:
for he is a babe.
Hebrews 5:12-13

How important it is to complete each step faithfully,
in order to become productive
in one's Christian life and service.

Soliloquy #458

Feelings of Rejection?

The memories of the past week-end are still fresh in my mind.
How wonderful it is to be remembered by one's children!

However, I realize that not all people are so blessed.
There are people who probably were having feelings of rejection or
even loss amidst all the "hoop-la" concerning Mother's Day.

There was a time during the days that Jesus Christ was on earth
when He specifically stated that He was sent
only to the lost sheep of the house of Israel.

Yet the Bible records an instance when He went to Galilee,
A Gentile woman who lived there came to Him
and pleaded for mercy and help for her daughter.

Jesus responded telling her that He was sent
only to the people of Israel.
He also told her that it wasn't right to take food
from the children and throw it to the dogs,
likening her to a dog. (Matt. 15:26)

However she continued to plead,
saying that what He said was true,
but even dogs got to eat scraps
that fell from their master's table.
So as usual, Jesus was moved by her faith.
He responded by granting her request.
The Bible records that her daughter was instantly healed.
(Matthew 15:21-28)

Perhaps at first the Gentile woman did have
feelings of rejection.

However, Jesus, true to His nature,
understood her plight and granted her need,
thereby lessening her feelings of rejection.

The Bible actually declares that Jesus came first
to the children of Israel.
However, in no unmistakable words,
it also declares:

*He came unto His own,
and His own receiveth Him not.
But as many as received Him
to them gave He power to become the sons of God,
even to them that believe on His name!
John 1:11-12*

Jesus was ready to help those who were in need.
He not only helped them,
but He gave His life to atone
for the sins of the whole world.
The apostle John wrote:

*He is the propitiation for our sins:
and not for ours only,
but for the sins of the whole world.
1 John 2:2*

There is no need for feelings of rejection
from our Heavenly Father.
Romans 10:13 states,

*For **whosoever** shall call upon
the name of the Lord shall be saved.*

Soliloquy # 459

Using the Scriptures

I was intrigued as I listened to the Word of God being expounded.
The teacher was beginning a series on First Thessalonians.
However, in order to get a better understanding,
it was important to see the background
of the Apostle Paul's ministry.

He turned to Acts, chapter 17.

Paul and Silas then traveled...
and came to Thessalonica,
where there was a Jewish synagogue.
As was Paul's custom,
he went to the synagogue service,
and for three Sabbaths in a row
he used the Scriptures....*(vss. 1-2)*

The apostle Paul was well-versed in the Old Testament,
for he had sat under Gamaliel, (Acts 22:3)
being taught the law of the Fathers.
So when he was converted,
he was able to do an extensive amount of searching
in those Scriptures in order to explain
what was happening at that time.
Thus, with his background, he was able to

*...**reason** with the people.*
*He **explained** the prophecies*
*and **proved** that the Messiah must suffer*
and rise from the dead. He said,
This Jesus I'm telling you about is the Messiah.
(vss. 2-3)

However, though some of the Jews and Greeks,
as well as prominent women, listened carefully and believed,
there were troublemakers who turned against Paul & Silas
and their message, causing riots.
So the believers helped them to escape.
They then went to Berea where they found that the people,

*...were more open-minded
than those in Thessalonica,
and they listened eagerly to Paul's message.
They **searched the Scriptures day after day**
to see if Paul and Silas were teaching the truth.
As a result, many Jews believed,
as did many of the prominent Greek women and men.
(vss.11-12)*

What was intriguing to me
were the techniques that Paul used in his ministry.
He was taught by a "master-teacher (Gamaliel),
and had learned well.
So he *reasoned,*
explained,
and *proved from the Scriptures*
that Jesus was the Messiah.

I thought,

'I must keep meditating daily on the Scriptures,
for they are God's Word.
Then I will be better equipped to follow
the example of the Apostle Paul
in order to reason, explain, and prove
that Jesus is Who He claimed to be.'

Soliloquy # 460

Winds of Devastating Force

The crash of thunder startled me!
The winds were causing the trees
to bend violently under their force.

My mind went back to the images that
I had seen on the television the day before.
The devastation of the tornado
in the Midwest was unimaginable.
People roamed around the rubbish
helplessly searching for any object
that might look familiar to them.
It was heartbreaking to watch.

I thought of Job in the Old Testament. He said,

O remember that my life is wind:
mine eye shall no more see good.
Job 7:7

He must have felt completely helpless,
unable to do anything about the tragedies around him.

Yet, he knew his Creator God,
and he still blessed His name. He said,

Naked came I out of my mother's womb,
and naked shall I return thither:
the LORD gave,
and the LORD hath taken away;
blessed be the name of the LORD.
Job 1:21

Another wise man mused, (Proverbs 30:4),

Who hath ascended up into heaven, or descended?
Who hath gathered the wind in his fists?
Who hath bound the waters in a garment?
Who hath established all the ends of the earth?
What is his name, and what is his son's name,
if thou canst tell?

But verse 5 continues:

Every word of God is pure:
He is a shield unto them
that put their trust in him.

As I read those verses,
I thought again of the destitute people in the Midwest.
One man said He prayed to the LORD,
and was able to take shelter under an object that had fallen.
He had to be dug out, but he was grateful to be alive.

In another instance,
a teacher said that when the tornado was hitting her school,
she was sheltering the children around her
and she did what she was not allowed to do.
She prayed!
And she and her students were saved
amidst all of the rubble around them!

One never knows when winds might blow
with devastating force.

Life is short,
but eternity is forever!

Soliloquy #461

Whatever things....

There are times
when God's Word lays heavy on my heart.
Today was such a day.

Someone was upset over grievances
she had held against someone for years.
Now those distorted memories seemed to smolder inside of her
causing her great anguish and pain, even bringing tears.

How much better it would have been for her
to give those grievances to the Lord.
He is the One Who is the Righteous Judge.
He will set all things right some day.
He keeps accurate records.

Meanwhile for peace of mind,
the Bible has the answer:

Whatsoever things are true,

Whatsoever things are honest, (honorable)

Whatsoever things are just, (right)

Whatsoever things are pure,

Whatsoever things are lovely,

Whatsoever things are of good report; (good repute)

if there be any virtue, (excellence)

and if there be any praise, (things worthy of praise)

think on these things.

Philippians 4:8

Sometime later in the day,
another instance brought this same verse to mind.

There was a text message on my cell phone:

"Please pray for God to watch over me."

This deeply touched my heart
since it felt as if the request held deep pain.

So for the next hour,
that person was in my prayers.

Philippians 4:8, ...*Whatever things...!*

I thanked the Lord for this Word.

Soliloquy # 462

An Amazing Prayer

We...do not cease to pray for you,

Oh, how good that would have felt
for the Colossian believers to hear these words!

It always meant so much to me
to be assured of my Mom's prayers.

The apostle Paul continued by telling them
specifically about his prayer for them:

*and to desire that ye might be filled
with the knowledge of his will.*

How important it is to have knowledge of God's will...

in all wisdom and spiritual understanding;

How often I pray for wisdom for myself and for others...

*That ye might walk worthy of the Lord
unto all pleasing,*

Oh yes! This is my most earnest desire!

being fruitful in every good work,

How wonderful to be fruitful always
in my work for the Lord!

and increasing in the knowledge of God;

This will come from my daily meditations in God's Word.

*Strengthened with all might,
according to his glorious power,*

His incredible, experiential power
is also available to strengthen me!

*unto all patience and longsuffering
with joyfulness.
Colossians 1:9-11*

Patience and Longsuffering with Joyfulness.

Might I experience this prayer.

It's evident it is possible.

Soliloquy # 463

The Sun is Shining!

I was sitting on my sofa
and happened to glance outside...

I saw the sun shining,
and heard the birds singing!

My heart and mind began to echo
the following thoughts....

The sun is shining,
The birds are singing,
All seems quite right in my world.

God's world was perfect,
His love was reaching
To all who would receive it.

But man came and sinned
God's love was still there,
He sent His only loved Son.

Jesus came and lived,
He loved and served them,
Until they crucified Him.

But God's love's still there,
Reaching all who came,
Offering them salvation.

This gift is for all
Who accept His Son,
Promising Life Eternal!

God's SON is always shining!

Soliloquy #464

Celebrating our Liberty

Our nation's pledge of allegiance
is something that I have cherished from my childhood days
when, as a student, I recited it from memory.
It has never left me without deep emotional vibrations.

The section that comes to mind today is as follows:

"One nation under God,
indivisible,
with liberty
and justice for all."

As our country will be celebrating
the day of our independence
with picnics, potlucks, parties, and fireworks,
I was prompted to think of the liberty
that I have in the Lord Jesus Christ!

What makes this so significant is that it was not always so.
Our position as Gentiles was not a privileged one,
nor did we always have this liberty in Christ.
The Jewish nation had been God's chosen people,
the privileged ones.
Gentiles were secondary citizens.

But God in His mercy called a man
by the name of Saul of Tarsus (later called Paul),
and told him that he would be His chosen vessel
"to take His message to the Gentiles and to kings,
as well as to the people of Israel." (Acts 9:15)

What an amazing transformation that would have been in his day!
As a result of obeying God's calling,
the apostle Paul suffered unimaginably.

But he obeyed God's call.
As a result, today, even as a Gentile,
I am privileged to be considered one of God's children.
For Ephesians 3:6 states:

And this is God's plan:
Both Gentiles and Jews
who believe the Good News
share equally in the riches
inherited by God's children.
Both are part of the same body,
and both enjoy the promise of blessings
because they belong to Christ Jesus.
Ephesians 3:6-7 (NLT)

This gives me unbelievable liberty, freedom, and a blessed hope.

Secondly, because of our country's
declaration of independence
that we will be celebrating this week,
I have complete freedom and liberty to worship God.
Previously the organized church dictated the worship.
Even today, some countries still dictate the forms of religion.

I'm very thankful that I have
the freedom and liberty to worship God
according to the dictates of my heart.

Soliloquy # 465

A Blessed Relationship

I feel very blessed because this past week
my son and daughter have been with me.
My other daughter seems to be with me also because,
even though she is many miles away,
we keep in close contact by phone and email every day.
But meanwhile, my son and daughter's presence
fills me with great contentment!

What a wonderful mystical relationship
there exists between a mother and child,
no matter how old they might become!

When I think of my relationship
with my parents or with my children,
it helps me understand more fully
the relationship that I have with my Heavenly Father.
The Bible has no lack of references
regarding this special relationship.

For example,

*For you are all children of God
through faith in Christ Jesus.
Galatians 3:26*

What a special privileged feeling it is to be a child of God!

The Bible spells out what my behavior patterns
as a child of God should be,
just as parents would instruct their children.

*Imitate God, therefore, in everything you do,
because you are his dear children.
Ephesians 5:1*

However,
it is possible to wander away from God
and not obey Him,
just as some children wander away
from the instructions of their parents.
But how ashamed they could become
when they are reconciled once again?
The Bible warns about this too:

*And now dear children,
remain in fellowship with Christ
so that when he returns,
you will be full of courage
and not shrink back from him in shame.
1 John 2:28*

How deeply it thrills my heart when I can say:

*I have no greater joy
than to hear that my children
walk in the truth.
3 John 4*

Soliloquy # 466

Startling Thoughts

It was a bit shocking the first time
that I went over a road that was being patched.

A couple of feet to my right,
there was a hole, about 7 or 8 feet deep,
with a pipe running near the bottom of it.

A workman was in the hole working on the pipe.

It did startle me for a minute, for it brought to mind
an image that I had seen of a car down in a 'sink hole'.

Evidently the road had suddenly collapsed
trapping the car down in the hole.

Later, as I was thinking of the reality of everything
that must be going on under the ground
where we move and live,
the whole complex of the underground
rail system in England came to my mind.

It is beyond belief that all
of that whole system could be taking place
right under the ground where people are living!

Well, I thought to myself, in a microscopic way,
isn't it amazing to think of everything
that is going on in my body, right under my skin?

It covers a multitude of very important systems...
and I simply take them all for granted,
never giving them a second thought.

When I do stop to think especially about every part
of my circulatory and respiratory systems,

I marvel over the thought
that it is all involuntary,
constantly working in spite
of what I might be doing or thinking.

The Psalmist wrote:

I will praise thee:
for I am fearfully and wonderfully made:
marvellous are thy works;
and that my soul knoweth right well.
Psalm 139:14

It is indeed amazing to think of everything
that goes on in my body and in my world
without any thought of mine.

How marvelous are the works of the LORD!

Soliloquy # 467

Receiving God's Rest

As I was reading through the historical books
in the Old Testament,
I began to feel weary over the endless battles
the children of Israel had
as they defended their homes and families.

But after many years of battles
while they were under the reign of King David,
they finally were able to have **rest**.

Then David challenged them to build a sanctuary
for the LORD God.

He told them:

*Is not the LORD your God with you
and hath he not given you **rest** on every side?*

*For he hath given the inhabitants
of the land into mine hand;
and the land is subdued
before the LORD,
and before his people.
1 Chronicles 22:18*

David collected the materials,
and his son, Solomon,
had the magnificent sanctuary built.

However, their **rest** did not last,
for after a while they rebelled against the Lord their God.
And once again they had battles to fight.

Then God told them:

*Stand ye in the ways, and see,
and ask for the old paths,
where is the good way, and walk therein,
and ye shall find **rest** for your souls.
But they said, We will not walk therein.
Jeremiah 6:16*

When Jesus was on earth,
He had a similar message.
And thankfully,
it still rings true even today,

*Come unto me,
all ye that labour
and are heavy laden,
and I will give you **rest**.*

*Take my yoke upon you, and learn of me;
for I am meek and lowly in heart:
and ye shall find **rest** unto your souls.
Matthew 11:28-29 (KJV)*

It is a choice that people have to make
in order to receive his rest.

Soliloquy # 468

The Squirrel in the Tree

Last night as I was sitting in my comfy chair reading,
I glanced out the window to rest my eyes.

A grayish squirrel dashed up a tree,
stopped, and furtively scanned all directions.
He seemed satisfied that there was no danger nearby,
so he continued scampering up the tree
until he stopped on a narrow branch.
He slithered on it, stretching himself out,
seeming to become one with the branch.
I could hardly tell where the squirrel ended
and the branch began!

As he rested,
I went back to my Kindle to continue reading.
But instead, my eyes drifted back out the window to see
if my friend 'Squirrel' was still there.
Strangely, I could not see him anywhere.

I scanned all the branches in that area
but he was no where to be found.

When I concentrated on the branch where he had been,
I thought that it did seem a little thicker than I remembered,
but there was absolutely no definite shape or movement there.

So I surmised that he had gone somewhere else.
I looked around for him, puzzled how he had gone that quickly.

Suddenly, that branch seemed to peel away as I watched.

It *was* my Squirrel!

He had effectively camouflaged himself
to become one with the branch.

The amazing ability that God has given
to all his little creatures
to hide from their enemies
continues to amaze me.

What a gracious and wise Creator we worship!

Jesus said,

Are not two sparrows sold for a copper coin?
And not one of them falls to the ground
apart from your Father's will.

But the very hairs of your head
are all numbered.

Do not fear therefore;
you are of more value
than many sparrows.
Matthew 10:29 (NKJV)

As God cares for the tiny sparrows
and all His little creatures,
how much more will He care for His children!

Soliloquy 469

Is This God's Will?

"There have been so many bad things happening,"
someone exclaimed.
"How can such things be God's will?"

Isaiah 55:8-9 records God's words:

*For my thoughts are not your thoughts,
neither are your ways my ways, saith the Lord.*

But does this mean that He takes pleasure
in sending me 'bad things?'
My innermost being exclaims,
'No! That can never be the case!'

How can I be so sure about that?

First of all
I believe that the Bible is God's Word.
Psalm 139 graphically illustrates
how much interest He has in me.

Secondly,
the Bible is full of examples
illustrating how God overruled in people's lives,
showing how He turned bad things
into what turned out for good (Romans 8:28).

For example, Joseph was beloved of his father,
yet his brothers hated him and sold him to passing merchants
who took him and sold him as a slave.

He endured all kinds of injustices, but eventually,
he became the 'right hand man' to the Pharaoh.

Genesis 50 records Joseph telling his brothers,
'You intended to harm me,
but God intended it all for good!'

The book of Job reveals Satan wanting to attack Job
to show that the reason for his righteousness
was because of God's blessing.

God responded by consenting to 'lower the hedge' around Job.
So Satan did his dirty work, yet Job continued to praise God.
In the end, God blessed Job and gave him more
than he had in the beginning.

The Bible gives many examples of people who loved God,
yet they endured all kinds of trials and testings
(Hebrews 11:32-40).
They were confident of God's presence and blessing in the end.

Thirdly,
2 Corinthians 1:3-4 is especially good
for me to remember whenever I encounter trials and testings;
it has proven so true:

Blessed be God,
even the Father of our Lord Jesus Christ,
the Father of mercies, and the God of all comfort;
Who comforteth us in all our tribulation,
that we may be able to comfort them
which are in any trouble,
by the comfort wherewith we ourselves
are comforted of God.

Soliloquy #470

Exercise Thyself Unto...?

As I was doing my exercises this morning,
the Bible verse from 1 Timothy 4:7
came into my mind:

Exercise thyself unto godliness...

Probably exercising is not a favorite thing
for most people to do,
but there is usually a reason or a goal
they have in mind that keeps them striving.
In order to reduce back pain,
I exercise my back in order to strengthen it.

My niece and nephew are in California
coaching their swim team this week.
Before those young people even thought
of going to the 'Nationals'
they had to practice and do exercises
to strengthen their bodies.
It took many hours of consistent effort on their parts
and finally all of their perseverance paid off.
They became local, then regional champions,
finally making the goal of going to the nationals.

The Scriptures graphically illustrate the principle
that there needs to be a consistent development.

The Apostle Paul said he was striving
like an athlete toward his goal;

God also knew mankind needed an example to follow.
So He sent His beloved Son, Jesus,

Who though He was God,

took on human flesh and lived among mankind
so that people would know what it was like
to be more 'God-like'.

*Let us run with endurance the race
God has set before us.
We do this by keeping our eyes on Jesus,
the champion who initiates
and perfects our faith.
Hebrews 12:1-2*

Might I exercise myself with this goal,
not only with this life in view,
but also toward the next, keeping in mind, 1 Timothy 4:8,

*...godliness is profitable unto all things,
having promise of the life that now is,
and of that which is to come.*

As I exercise myself toward being more 'God-like',
I pray as did Eliza Hewitt,

*More about Jesus would I know,
More of His grace to others show
More of His saving fullness see
More of His love who died for me.*

Soliloquy # 471

Heartfelt Praise!

This morning I was filled with heartfelt praise to the Lord!

My heart is still overflowing
with thankfulness
for once again the Lord
showered His loving-kindnesses
and tender mercies upon us all!

My 100 pound granddaughter insisted as usual
on having her baby at home completely natural.
Since this is her fifth pregnancy,
there was not as much apprehension
until I saw how huge she was getting!
She eventually gave birth to a 10 pound daughter!

Needless to say,
I was in prayer almost constantly for them,
and once again, the Lord answered my prayers.
Thankfully, both mother and baby have been fine.

Mommy and Daddy named her 'Faith Christine'
which means 'Faith, a little follower of Christ.'

So today as I read the following prayer
in the book of Nehemiah,
my heart joined in the praise,

May your glorious name be praised!
May it be exalted above all blessing and praise!

You alone are the LORD.

*You made the skies
and the heavens
and all the stars.
You made the earth
and the seas
and everything in them.
You preserve them all,
and the angels of heaven worship you.*

*...you have done what you promised,
for you are always true to your word.
Nehemiah 9:5-6*

*You are a God of forgiveness,
gracious and merciful,
slow to become angry,
and rich in unfailing love.
Nehemiah 9:17*

Soliloquy # 472

Similes About my LORD

As I was reading Psalm 36:5-7 again,
my meditations flowed along like a river
with the Psalmist as he penned
the following satisfying similes,

*Your unfailing love, O LORD,
is as vast as the heavens;*

Oh, how true this is to me –
I look at the vastness of the heavens
deeper than the eye or even the telescope can see
– and I marvel over the unfailing love of my LORD!

Your faithfulness reaches beyond the clouds.

His faithfulness is beyond measure...
How true this has proven to be, time after time!

*"Your righteousness is like the mighty mountains,
Your justice is like the ocean depths."*

How wonderful to rest assured in the fact that
the Lord's righteousness and justice knows no end!

*You care for people and animals alike, O LORD.
How precious is your unfailing love, O God!*

How amazing is God's unfailing love,
it is definitely a precious thought indeed!

*All humanity finds shelter
in the shadow of your wings.*

I appreciate the metaphor
of the hen shielding her chicks under her wings
because it makes me feel completely safe
and content with the LORD!

William O. Cushing penned the words
to a well-loved song,

Under His wings, I am safely abiding,
Though the night deepens and tempests are wild,
Still I can trust Him, I know He will keep me,
He has redeemed me, and I am His child

Under His wings, under His wings,
Who from His love can sever?
Under His wings my soul shall abide,
Safely abide forever.

Soliloquy # 473

Christ Jesus: My Strength

Someone told me about a little gal
who was quite apprehensive
about going into Boot Camp.

Evidently, she had tried to get a job, but couldn't.
So her father wanted her to go into Boot Camp.

The person who told me about the girl
asked for Scriptures that might help her.
She said that the young girl was visibly upset
and quite nervous about it.

One of the verses
that has come to mean a lot for me
in many difficult situations,
and has given me great assurance
is Philippians 4:19,

*My God shall supply all your needs
according to his riches in glory
in Christ Jesus.*

Then as that verse gives me
the assurance that I need,
my mind quickly tells me that,

*I can do all things through Christ
Who strengthens me!
Philippians 4:13*

How thankful I am for God's Word,
for it is a firm foundation
upon which I can stand!

I know that,
Thy Word is truth.
John 17:7

and I have experienced,

Thy Word is a lamp unto my feet,
and a light unto my path.
Psalm 119:105

Definitely, God's Word has been my light
pointing the way to my Savior,
Jesus Christ,
Who strengthens me
and gives me assurance!

Soliloquy # 474

The Music of the Earth

How fascinating it is to think
of the music that our earth holds!

I understand that scientists have found
that the earth is 'humming'.

For example, they say that the sun makes sounds.
I can hear the sounds that the churning ocean makes,
even the trees seem to whisper
and make music in the breezes.
The pictures on the weather maps
show the rolling atmosphere,
that also must make some sounds.

Evidently, the stones and rocks
could make some sounds,
for when Jesus was on earth,
He was riding on a colt towards Jerusalem.
People spread their clothes on the road
praising God with a loud voice
for all the mighty works they had seen.

However, the religious leaders of the day
called to Jesus and told Him
to rebuke the people.

But He answered them:

*I tell you that if these should keep silent,
the stones would immediately cry out.
Luke 19:40*

The Psalmist exclaimed,

Let the heavens be glad, and let the earth rejoice;
let the sea roar, and all that fills it;
let the field exult, and everything in it!
Then shall all the trees of the forest sing for joy
Psalm 96:11-12

While I was thinking of all these things,
it occurred to me that it is not so unusual
to imagine a scene in the future
of a great symphony of all of God's creation
joining in with all mankind praising the LORD God!

For the Bible predicts:

God has highly exalted Him
and given Him the name
which is above every name,

that at the name of Jesus
every knee should bow,...

and that every tongue should confess
that Jesus Christ is Lord,
to the glory of God the Father.
Romans 2:9-11

Soliloquy # 475

The Greatness of our Creator

I am still glowing in the reminders
of the music of the earth,
for everywhere I look and in every place I go,
I smile as I think of the presence
of the LORD in His creation!

A friend reminded me of an instance
where the LORD God actually used
His creation to guide His people!

It is recorded in 2 Samuel 5.

The Philistines seemed to be constantly going
against David and his people.
But when they did,
David sought the LORD's guidance.

The LORD sometimes used His creation
to tell him what he should do,

*David inquired of the LORD,
and He said,*

*You shall not go up;
circle around behind them,
and come upon them
in front of the mulberry trees.*

*And it shall be,
when you hear the sound of marching
in the tops of the mulberry trees,*

then you shall advance quickly.
for then the LORD will go out before you
to strike the camp of the Philistines.
2 Samuel 5:23-24

And that's exactly what happened.
Each time they sought the LORD,
the battle was won!

So as the little birds sing their songs,
and other birds screech, quack, and honk;
As the wind whistles through the trees,
and rustles through the bushes;
As the ocean roars, crashes,
or laps gently on the shore;
I hear the sounds of the LORD my God.

The heavens declare the glory of God
And the firmament shows His handiwork.
Day unto day utters speech,
And night unto night reveals knowledge.
Psalm 19:1-2

If creation is so great...
how much greater is our Creator!

Soliloquy # 476

'Unsolvable' Problems?

My Mom used to tell me,
"Every family has its own cross to bear."

Her statement has come to mind recently,
for it seems that there are so many friends
who are experiencing problems,
many of which are very serious.

But are they unsolvable problems?
I don't think so.

A close friend of ours has often exclaimed:

There are no problems, only opportunities!

But what about the person who thinks
that the present problem is really
more than he can handle?

Once again, as I turn to Holy Scripture,
I realize that God's Word can advise,
and there is a solution.

*Trust in the LORD with all thine heart
and lean not on thine own understanding.*

In all thy ways, acknowledge Him
and He shall direct thy path.
Proverbs 3:5-6

It brings great comfort
to know that the LORD can direct my path,

However, there is a condition that must be met.
It is that in everything
I must acknowledge and trust the LORD.

The words of Jesus
can be applied also when He said:

Seek ye first the kingdom of God
and His righteousness
and all these things
shall be added unto you.
Matthew 6:33

C.S. Lewis, in a nutshell,
commented on this verse:

"Put first things first
and we get second things thrown in:
Put second things first
and we lose both first and second things."

Soliloquy # 477

My Creator God Speaks!

How interesting that at several times during the past week,
references to God's handiwork came to my attention.

For example,
in the book of Isaiah, the prophet declared:

*God, the LORD, created the heavens
and stretched them out.
He created the earth and everything in it.
He gives breath to everyone,
life to everyone who walks the earth...
Isaiah 42:5*

And lest anyone missed God's message,
Isaiah repeated,

*This is what the LORD says--
your Redeemer and creator.
I am the LORD who made all things.
I alone stretched out the heavens.
Isaiah 44:24*

The second coincidence occurred while I was with a friend.
She had a CD recording of waves washing upon the shore.
I felt totally relaxed, almost mesmerized, while listening.

Then what clinched the experiences
was when my daughter and I visited the beach.
The repetitive sound of the waves nearly put us to sleep,
It all made a profound impression.

'Yes,' I thought,
' The Lord is the One Who spoke,

not only through the prophet,
but also He spoke
through the vastness of His creation.'

It seems to create a cocoon-like wrap around my mind.
Whenever I think, feel, and hear it,
it gives me an incredible sense of peace.

O LORD, my God, when I in awesome wonder
consider all the worlds Thy hands have made.
I see the stars, I hear the rolling thunder.
Thy power throughout the universe displayed....

Then sings my soul...How Great Thou art!

Soliloquy # 478

Uncertain Future?

The future is full of uncertainty these days...

Our president stated this morning
that he is unwilling to negotiate.

The congress has been at their 'wit's end'
to present other solutions.

A government shutdown is on the horizon.
(Maybe that would be a good idea
so our local officials could begin
to solve our own problems.)

Meanwhile,
there is a hurricane brewing
in the Gulf of Mexico;
it is heading straight for us.

Our mobile home park's caretaker
is walking around warning people
to have an evacuation plan in place.

Our daughter, who lives next door to us,
takes it lightly --
she told me
that she'd like to go to the Gulf to watch it!

It is definitely a time of uncertainty!
So what about my future?
That is secure, because...
I am positively persuaded that
it is as bright as the promises of God!

And what are they?

*Trust in the Lord with all thine heart,
and lean not on thine own understanding.*

*In all thy ways acknowledge him,
and He shall direct thy paths!
Proverbs 3:5-6*

*My God shall supply all your needs
according to His riches in glory
by Christ Jesus.
Philippians 4:19*

*We know that all things
work together for good,
to them that love God,
to them who are called
according to His purpose.
Romans 8:28*

On these matters,
there is no uncertainty,
because my trust and hope
lie in God Who cannot lie!

Soliloquy #479

The Faithfulness of God!

After the stormy winds blew
and the rains stopped,
I opened the window
and smelled the wonderful fresh air.

The cheerful sound of the birds singing
brought peace and joy to my soul.

It was impossible not to pause
and thank the Lord for His faithfulness!

The words of the hymn writer,
Thomas Chisholm,
captured my thoughts:

Summer and winter and springtime and harvest
Sun, moon, and stars in their courses above,
Join with all nature in manifold witness,
To Thy great faithfulness, mercy, and love.

Great is Thy faithfulness!
Morning by morning new mercies I see
All I have needed Thy hand hath provided
Great is Thy faithfulness, Lord unto me!

Recently I heard a pastor speaking
about the faithfulness of God,
so this attribute of God
was at the forefront of my mind.

As I searched the Scriptures about this matter,
a paraphrase of 2 Timothy 2:11-13 came to mind:

*If we die with Him,
we will also live with Him.*

*If we endure hardship,
we will reign with Him.*

*If we deny Him,
He will deny us.*

If we are unfaithful,
He remains faithful,
for He cannot deny who He is!

Yes! God Is Faithful!
Therefore my source of strength is in Him!

Somehow the calming sound of the little birds
reminded me of the blessed assurances
of God's great faithfulness
and I said a little prayer of thanks to Him.

Soliloquy # 480

A Happy Face!

What a difference it makes
when I 'put on a happy face!'

My mind can do amazing things...
even when I am hurting.

If I put on a happy face,
it seems to brighten not only myself,
but everyone around me seems happier also!

In fact,
I smile thinking of the song,

Put on a happy face.

Gray skies are gonna clear up
Put on a happy face
Brush off the clouds and cheer up
Put on a happy face....

Wipe off the "full of doubt" look,
Slap on a happy grin!
And spread sunshine all over the place
Just put on a happy face.

The Scriptures go even further.
They go so far as to infer
that my mental outlook
impacts my physical well-being.

A wise man gave insightful thoughts:

*A cheerful heart is good medicine,
but a broken spirit saps a person's strength.
Proverbs 17:22*

*A glad heart makes a happy face;
a broken heart crushes the spirit.
Proverbs 15:13*

It is possible to "put on a happy face,"
especially when I experience the truth
found in the Holy Scriptures,
such as:

*Now may the Lord of peace himself
give you his peace
at all times
and in every situation.
The Lord be with you all.
2 Thessalonians 3:16*

Soliloquy # 481

All Your Anxiety

I recently heard a speaker
whose topic was Anxiety.
He had many good thoughts
and cited numerous Scriptures.

However, all of a sudden,
he realized that the time allotted
for his message was gone.

Yet he felt compelled to share
a myriad of Scriptures that he had studied..

So he simply read the list of references that he had
and said they could be found on his web page.

Later in the week,
the topic of Anxiety came back to my mind,
and with it came a chorus I had long forgotten....

*All your anxiety, all your care,
take to the mercy seat
leave it there.
Never a burden He cannot bear
Never a friend like Jesus.*

As the little chorus stayed with me,
it caused me to realize the truth of those words.

It does make a difference
when I heed its advice,
because of what the Scriptures advise:

Casting all your care upon Him:
for He careth for you.
1 Peter 5:7

Regardless of when any care might arise,

the peace that He promises
flows over my anxiety,

flooding my mind,

leaving in its wake
His perfect peace

leaving me contented
and grateful.

Soliloquy # 482

Clouds

The striking contrast between
the white cumulus clouds
and the cerulean blue sky
makes my heart speed up
rejoicing in the beauty
and artistic wonder
of God's creation!

As a child,
often I would imagine various pictures
that seemed to appear in the formation of the clouds!

At times, I saw various animals.

At other times a pathway would appear
leading up to the throne of God!

This was always exciting for me
as I placed myself into the picture.

Now as I contemplate the oft-repeated mention
of clouds in the Holy Scriptures,
my soul seems to overwhelm
my consciousness with longing
as I place myself once again in the clouds
rising to meet the Lord in the air!

The following passage has probably given
the most intense feeling
and well-timed and thankful comfort:

*For if we believe that Jesus died and rose again,
even so, them also which sleep in Jesus
will God bring with him.*

*For this we say unto you
by the word of the Lord:
that we which are alive and remain
shall not prevent them which are asleep.*

*For the Lord himself
shall descend from heaven
with a shout,
with the voice of the archangel,
and with the trump of God:*

*and the dead in Christ
shall rise first:*

*Then we which are alive and remain
shall be caught up together with them
in the clouds,
to meet the Lord in the air:*

and so shall we ever be with the Lord.

1 Thessalonians 4:14-17

Soliloquy #483

Acts of Kindness

Acts of kindness are not always rewarded in this life,
in fact, some people seem to take them for granted,
sometimes causing misunderstanding
and even producing hard feelings.

However, when I think of loving acts of kindness,
I think of my dear younger sister.

Her thoughtful ways make me thank the Lord
for her consistent winsome character.
She is conscious of people in need
and offers her help in various ways:

For example, an elderly couple needed to be transported
back farther south from their summer home up north,
(a trip of over 500 miles one way).

So my sister and her husband offered to drive them.
The journey meant loss of work and extra costs for them,
plus the fact that they drove back the next day
making it a physically and emotionally tiring experience.
I was overwhelmed with their kindness.

Another example:
an older single lady calls her on Sunday mornings
and tells her that she "can pick me up for church."
It involves signing her out of her Nursing Home,
helping her into the car,
and then putting her wheel-chair in the back.

Every Wednesday, she and some other friends
go to her Nursing home for "coffee."
Sometimes they decide to go to a restaurant

so she will be able to "get out."
So my sister picks the handicapped lady up,
wheel-chair and all, and joins the others.

Thirdly, whenever someone has had surgery
or has some other need,
my sister makes a dinner for them,
complete with dessert.
Then she and her husband deliver it
to the shut-in's home.

As I was thinking of her many acts of kindness,
which often go on without any thanks,
I thought of the following Scripture:

For God is not unrighteous
to forget your work
and labour of love,
which ye have shewed toward his name,
in that ye have ministered to the saints,
and do minister.
Hebrews 6:10

Soliloquy # 484

Are You OK?

As the images on TV project the horrible devastation
that has remained from the huge typhoon
in the Philippine Islands,
my heart keeps crying out,
'Are you OK?'

The cause of my burden
is mainly because our beloved friend
and national pastor lives and ministers there.

Years ago our church brought him
to the USA to share his burden.

During that time he was a great blessing
to everyone wherever he ministered.
We could not help but love and admire him.

However, my lovely daughter reminds me,
"Mom, he'll be right there in the middle of it all
helping to meet their needs."

I'm sure she is right, being the way he is,
he would be doing all he could to help.

But then the question comes up
that so many people repeatedly ask,
"Why does God allow so many bad things to happen?"

My mind drifted to our Sunday evening prayer service.
There were so many people with serious needs:

Some with homelessness looming on the horizon,
some with serious physical, emotional, and spiritual needs,
some with recent deaths of loved ones,
some losing jobs, pastors losing their way,
churches losing their pastors,
and the list goes on and on.

The needs were many,
but the Bible reminds me that the world
as it stands right now
is not the way that God originally created it,
nor is it the way that it will ultimately be.

And I saw a new heaven and a new earth:
for the first heaven and the first earth
were passed away.
Revelation 21:1

But before this happens, there will be perilous times,
there will be famines, and pestilences,
and earthquakes in divers places.
(2 Timothy 3:1; Mat. 24:7)

Such disasters could serve as warnings
of the coming day of the LORD,
but there is salvation for those who seek the LORD.

Seek ye the LORD....
it may be ye shall be hid
in the day of the LORD's anger.
Zephaniah 2:3

Soliloquy # 485

"In Everything Give Thanks"

Every day my lovely granddaughter has been recording
something for which she has been thankful.
And I have been very impressed!

Then I remembered that the Bible instructs me to be...

*Always giving thanks
to God the Father for everything,
in the name of our Lord Jesus Christ.
Ephesians 5:20*

So I thought to myself,
that is what I will do also.
As I started, it was easy;
however before I got very far,
I realized that there were some things
that didn't cause me to be thankful.

But that shouldn't be the case,
for I know the Scriptures clearly state
that I should be giving thanks for *everything!*
Actually most of the time it is easy to be thankful,
but sometimes doing it seems to be quite difficult.

Well, I knew that I needed to check the Scriptures again,
and found that without a doubt it should indeed be my aim.
For as if that previous verse were not clear enough,
the theme of giving thanks is repeated all through the Bible:

*In every thing give thanks
for this is the will of God
in Christ Jesus for you.
1 Thessalonians 5:18*

It wasn't long before I realized
that in every difficult situation,
though it might be hard at first,
there is always much for which I can be thankful.

As Romans 8:38-39 came to mind,
everything seemed to diminish into insignificance!

*For I am persuaded that neither death, nor life,
nor angels, nor principalities, nor powers,
nor things present, nor things to come,
nor height, nor depth,
nor any other creature,
shall be able to separate us
from the love of God,
which is in Christ Jesus our Lord .*

Soliloquy # 486

The God of Hope

Thanksgiving has come and gone,
leaving precious memories of family members
and many friends who had joined together
to make these days a special occasion.

However, these times must come to an end,
because normal routines of life must once again resume.

As the Scriptures cite in Philippians 3:13,

*...forgetting what lies behind
and reaching forward
to what lies ahead...*

But what does 'lie ahead'?
Sometimes the future looks quite dismal these days.

If it were not for my faith in the Lord Jesus Christ,
I would certainly be discouraged.
As 1 Corinthians 15:19 (NAS) states:

*If we have hoped in Christ in this life only,
we are of all men most to be pitied.*

But on the contrary,
since God is my source of hope
or confident expectation,
sometimes in the midst of troubles and trials,
I can feel as if I am
overflowing with joy and peace
because of my complete trust in Him!

I pray that God,

the source of hope,

*will fill you completely
with joy and peace*

because you trust in him.

*Then you will overflow
with confident hope*

*through the power
of the Holy Spirit.*

Romans 15:13 (NLT)

This is my prayer for all my family and friends.

Soliloquy # 487

Unexpected Changes

How quickly and unexpectedly life can change!

My husband and I were preparing
to paint a ramp and handrails.

He was going to roll the paint on the ramp.
He had the long-handled roller and paint ready,
and I was going to paint the handrails while
standing on the ground next to the ramp.

All was going according to plan
when suddenly I turned for something,
tripped over stones and uneven ground,
and couldn't catch my balance.

The next thing I knew,
my face was sliding to a halt
in the twigs, grass, and stones.

The two middle fingers of my left hand
were trapped under the weight of my chest.

I remember thinking,
'How is it possible for those fingers
to bend so far backwards?'

I was helped to a sitting position,
while my daughter who was just leaving for work ran to me,
took my glasses off, tried to wipe my face, brushed my clothes,
and then ran to the house to get a frozen bag of veggies.

She put it on my face and hand.
I assured her that I was OK,
but she helped me inside so I could lie down.

'Well,' I thought, 'How quickly life can change.'

Several plans that my husband and I had made
now needed to be adjusted.

Circumstances in life can bring surprises,
our best-laid plans can so quickly come to an end.

*You do not know
what your life will be like tomorrow.
You are just a vapor
that appears for a little while
and then vanishes away.
James 4:14*

In spite of the unenexpected,

I trust in the Lord!

He promised to never desert me nor forsake me.
(Hebrews 13:5b)

Soliloquy # 488

Come to Worship Him

This time of year some people's thoughts
turn to the account of the birth of Jesus
as recorded in the Holy Scriptures.

*Now after Jesus was born
in Bethlehem of Judea
in the days of Herod the king,
behold magi from the east
arrived in Jerusalem, saying,
"Where is He who has been born King of the Jews?
For we have seen His star in the east,
and have come to worship Him."
Matthew 2:1-2*

These wise men spent their lives studying the stars.
So when this amazing star became visible,
they knew its significance.
and set out to find this King
who had been born.

They traveled a great distance to worship Him
because the Scriptures state
that when they found Him,
He was a young child (Matthew 2:11).

*"And they came into the house
and saw the Child with Mary His mother,
and they fell down and worshiped Him."*

Today true worship is far from the minds of most people
for He is often forgotten in the chaos of gift-giving,

Romans 12:1-2 suggests what is truly the way to worship Him:

*I plead with you to give your bodies to God
because of all He has done for you.*

*Let them be a living sacrifice--
the kind He will find acceptable.*

This is truly the way to worship Him.

*Don't copy the behavior and customs of this world,
but let God transform you into a new person
by changing the way you think....*

Wise men still seek Him!

Soliloquy #489

The Word Became Flesh

"The Word" has been staying in my mind lately.
What is its significance
and why can it not leave my mind?

I happened to read the first chapter of John
in a modern translation recently,
and the meaning of 'the Word'
caused my soul to be deeply touched.

Its significance grew
as I pondered these amazing things!

*In the beginning
the Word already existed.*

*The Word was with God,
and the Word was God.*

He existed in the beginning with God,

He always was!

God created everything through Him.

He was the Creator!

*The Word gave life to everything that was created,
and His life brought light to everyone.*

*The light shines in the darkness,
and the darkness can never extinguish it....*

*He came into the world He created,
but the world didn't recognize Him*

*He came to His own people,
and even they rejected Him.*

He came into the world as that little baby
Who grew up and was rejected, but...
thankfully it doesn't remain there...

*But to all who believed Him
and accepted Him,
He gave the right
to become the children of God....*

*The Word became human
and made His home among us.
John 1:1-5, 10-12, 14*

'The Word' is none other than Jesus Christ,
my Savior and Lord!

Soliloquy #490

The Enormity of it all!

I still cannot begin to fathom
the enormity of the fact
that God, the Creator of the universe
became human – a baby!
And He grew, lived, played,
worked among people,
and died for me.
But He rose from the dead
and sat at God's right hand.

*Great is the mystery of Godliness:
God was manifest in the flesh,
justified in the Spirit,
seen of angels,
Preached unto the Gentiles,
believed on in the world,
received up into glory.
1 Timothy 3:16*

How amazing is it that
He is now seated at God's right hand
living and making intercession for even me!

*It is Christ that died, yea rather,
that is risen again,
who is even at the right hand of God,
who also maketh intercession for us.
Romans 8:34*

This warms my heart as nothing else can,
especially since I injured my hand
and broke my finger a few weeks ago.

The Orthopedic Surgeon put my hand in a cast
nearly up to my elbow,
which has made me feel quite useless.

Sometimes tears seem to be on the verge of breaking through.
especially when I seem to be unable to do even simple things.
It destroys my feeling of independence.
and of being a helper!

But the Scriptures also tell me in Hebrews 4:16...

*Let us therefore come boldly
unto the throne of grace,
that we may obtain mercy,
and find grace to help in time of need.*

So at those times
I cast myself on God,
my mediator, my Savior,

and I marvel anew over
the enormity of God becoming flesh,
and becoming my Savior,
always ready to help in my time of need!

Soliloquy # 491

Pause To Consider

I awakened out of breath from the struggles in my dream!
It seemed as if it were up to me
to get others out of some predicament
...and it seemed impossible!

Then I realized that it was a dream!

So I began to spend time in prayer
relaxing in the presence of the Lord.

The words of a famous speaker came to mind.
His oft repeated phrase insisted:
"Garbage in, garbage out"

I realized that when I allowed myself
to watch violence or unsettling things,
it seemed that some of those things
would stay in my subconscious
and would be ready to emerge
- usually in a dream!

Instead how much better it would be
if I would take my advice from God's Word:

Whatsoever things are true,
whatsoever things are honest,
whatsoever things are just,
whatsoever things are pure,
whatsoever things are lovely,
whatsoever things are of good report,

if there be any virtue,
and if there be any praise,

think on these things.
Philippians 4:8

As another new year is breaking,
and I pause to consider,
I realize that it is a good thing for me
to keep this passage in my mind.

My prayer will continue:

Let the words of my mouth,
and the meditations of my heart
be acceptable in Thy sight,
O LORD, my strength, and my redeemer.
Psalm 19:14

Shirley's Soliloquy # 492

In This Life Only?

As I was thinking about my dear friend
whose Mom had recently passed
from this life into heaven,
the following verse came into my mind,
and it has been staying there.

*If in this life only we have hope in Christ,
we are of all men the most pitiable.
1 Corinthians 15:22*

Needless to say, she and her family
are deeply missing their loved one.

However, they are comforted in the knowledge
that she is no longer suffering,
but instead she is enjoying being
in the presence of her Savior!

My friends have trusted Christ
as their personal Savior,
and they have this 'hope'
...not the 'wishing it were true'
kind of hope...
No!

Instead, in the Biblical sense of the word,
they have the 'confident expectation'
of knowing that their loved ones,
who have already left this life,
are presently 'at home' with the Lord.

At times like this,
I think back to the time

when my own Mom went to be with the Lord.
It was hard realizing that she was no longer physically with us.

But my mind immediately began to visualize her in heaven,
rejoicing in the presence of her Savior,
receiving rest from her physical problems,
totally restored in mind and body.

Then my mind drifted to those who do not have this 'hope'
who can only think of their loved
decaying in the ground,
or maybe even enduring torturous suffering.
How difficult it must be for them!

I'm so grateful and thankful to God
that it is not in this life only that I have hope,
but also in the life to come!

One of my husband's friends said to him,
"Just think, if trusting Christ in this life is all there is,
it is still wonderful.

But if what we believe is really true,
then we've hit the jackpot!"

Soliloquy # 493

The Son that Shines Forever!

It was a fairly overcast sky,
gloomy clouds seemed to abound.

Then I opened my email and found
a note from a friend who wrote:

Life on this earth has its share of storms,
but heaven with the Son
that shines forever
is our hope.

How timely this note was on such a day as this!

Another friend had been having her "share of storms."
She sounded quite weighed down with it all.

During the time of this friend's trials and testings
I thought of the song written so long ago:

Never a trial that He is not there,
Never a burden that He doth not bear,
Never a sorrow that He doth not share,
Moment by moment, I'm under His care.

Moment by moment I'm kept in His love;
Moment by moment I've life from above;
Looking to Jesus till glory doth shine;
Moment by moment, O Lord, I am Thine.
    – Daniel W. Whittle, 1893

In addition to my thoughts about my friend,
this morning's challenge

with my injured hand
during occupational therapy
ground around in my head.

It seemed that I was straining
to work beyond my strength
when 'moment by moment
I'm kept in His love,
'moment by moment
I've life from above,'
gained consciousness.

I realized
that each moment here on earth
stretches right into eternity
as I look to Jesus
where I can rest in His glory
that will shine forever!

It is this confident expectation
that gives me strength
while here on earth!

Soliloquy # 494

An Amazing Testimony

Humble yourselves in the sight of the Lord,
and He will lift you up.
James 4:10

It was an amazing testimony!
He had been a pastor's son and he knew
that he had a certain amount of pride in his life.
He didn't want to humble himself before the Lord
and especially before the congregation
They had pretty much put him on a pedestal.

The story he told was heart-breaking:
His throat had shrunk in size to the extent
that he had been unable to eat solid food for 3 years
– even a grain of rice would make him gag.
His wife had to turn whatever food they had into liquid form.
He had been to several doctors
who had unsuccessfully tried everything.

However one Sunday evening, he was at the end of himself.
He knew that he had to humble himself before the Lord.
So after a tremendous struggle,
he walked up to the altar,
kneeled there,
and sought the Lord
with his heart broken and contrite:

The sacrifices of God are a broken spirit,
A broken and a contrite heart--
These, O God, You will not despise.
Psalm 51:17

He confessed his pride
and emptied himself,
giving all to the Lord.

And God touched his heart and made him whole.
He said he felt the Lord telling him
that his throat would be healed also.

After stopping at a restaurant with his family,
he ordered a meal.
His wife thought she'd have to take his meal home
and blend it for him as she always did.

However, to her amazement,
he was able to eat everything!

When this young man had finished
his testimony in church,
many people were touched
and tears were shed as they came to the altar
confessing their sins
and giving themselves totally to the Lord.

The LORD is near to those
who have a broken heart,
And saves such as have a contrite spirit.
Psalm 34:18

Soliloquy # 495

Knit Together by Love

My daughter stopped by to show me the lacy scarf
her friend from work had made for her.
It was a beautiful, intricate design.

As I thought about the amount of time
involved in forming each individual stitch,
I mused, 'It is definitely a work of love!'

Then I thought of the Scripture in Colossians
where the apostle Paul used the analogy of knitting!

He wanted everyone to be *"knit together in love."*

Because of my experience in knitting,
that was a striking visual for me.

The relationship of one stitch to another,
and even each twist and turn in forming each stitch
reinforced the concept of being tied integrally together!

The Scriptures record:

*I want you to know
how much I have agonized for you
...and for many other believers
who have never met me personally.*

*I want them to be encouraged
and* **knit together by strong ties of love.**

*I want them to have complete confidence
that they understand God's mysterious plan,
which is Christ himself.*

*In him lie hidden all the treasures
of wisdom and knowledge.
Colossians 2:2-3 (NLT)*

Didn't Jesus urge all His disciples
to show love for each other?

He said:

*By this all will know that you are My disciples,
if you have love for one another.
John 13:35*

Knitting will always remind me to be,

Knit together in LOVE!

Soliloquy # 496

Time Passes!

Time seems to have a way of getting away from me!

Every time I turn around,
it seems another week has passed!

So of course those weeks turn into a month,
and that often takes me by surprise!

I suppose it might be a part of growing older...
at least that's what I hear people say.

The Holy Scriptures have much to say
about the passing of time
and the need to live lives
that would be pleasing to the Lord--
especially as the days pass
and the time of His return draws near.

For example,
...Knowing the time,
that now it is high time to awake out of sleep;
for now our salvation is nearer
than when we first believed.

The night is far spent,
the day is at hand,.

Therefore let us cast off the works of darkness,
and let us put on the armor of light

Let us walk properly, as in the day,
...put on the Lord Jesus Christ....
Romans 13:11-14

The Scriptures not only urge believers
to practice right living,
but they also admonish us
to make the best use of time.

I appreciate how they do not mince words,
but clearly instruct us what to keep in mind.
For example,

*Walk in wisdom toward those who are outside,
redeeming the time, (buying up the time)*

*Let your speech always be with grace,
seasoned with salt,
that you may know
how you ought to answer each one.
Colossians 4:5-6*

Soliloquy # 497

Anticipation!

It's only a few days and I'll be headed to Texas!

All kinds of images fly into my mind when I mention Texas:
Cattle, Cowboys, Oil, Space Program, Ex-presidents;
and the vastness of its size (five times bigger than England)!

But now the images that gain major control of my mind
are my son, three of my granddaughters,
and all of their loved ones!

Even now, I can't keep a smile from my face
whenever I think of those five little great-grandchildren
and anticipate their hugs and happy faces!

Underneath and above all that excitement,
a warm feeling completely surrounds my heart.
Oh! How much they are all loved!
The anticipation of seeing them again
can be compared to nothing else.

My feelings remind me of how many
of my loved ones are now in heaven.
The anticipation of seeing them again
gives me great comfort.

As their faces flit into my memory,
I begin to name them one by one
and recall pleasant memories of times shared.

Anticipation is a wonderful thing!

The Bible says,

*Our perishable earthly bodies
must be transformed
into heavenly bodies
that will never die....*

*How we thank God,
who gives us victory over sin and death
through Jesus Christ our Lord!*

*So, my dear brothers and sisters,
be strong and steady,*

*"always enthusiastic about the Lord's work,
for you know that nothing you do
for the Lord is ever useless.*

1 Corinthians 15:53, 57-58

Soliloquy # 498

God Does Not Want...

My heart is deeply burdened for people
who think that life is meaningless
and when death comes,
that is the end.

Regardless of what they think, that is not the case!
The third chapter of 2 Peter (1-15) spells it out clearly,
first warning of scoffers who will not believe:

*First, I want to remind you that in the last days
there will be scoffers who will laugh at the truth
and do every evil thing they desire.*

This will be their argument:

*'Jesus promised to come back, did he?
Then where is he?
Why, as far back as anyone can remember,
everything has remained exactly the same
since the world was first created.'*

The Bible reminds people that
God made the heaven and earth,
and it declares that someday
everything will be consumed by fire.

*But you must not forget, dear friends,
that a day is like a thousand years to the Lord,
and a thousand years is like a day.*

*The Lord isn't really being slow
about the promise to return....*

No, he is being patient for your sake.

He does not want anyone to perish,
so he is giving more time for everyone to repent....

*Since everything around us is going to melt away,
what holy, godly lives you should be living!*

*....But we are looking forward to the new heavens
and new earth he has promised,
a world where everyone is right with God.*

*And so, dear friends,
while you are waiting for these things to happen,
make every effort to live a pure and blameless life.*

*And be at peace with God.
And remember, the Lord is waiting
so that people have time to be saved.*

2 Peter 3:3-4, 8-9, 11, 13-15

Soliloquy # 499

He Leadeth Me...

On our recent trip,
my husband and I saw unexpected situations,
the timing of which had to be more than coincidence.

As we looked back we realized that it was the Lord
once again leading through those difficult times.

My mind went to one of the many metaphors
in the book of John.

Probably one of my favorites is
Jesus as a Shepherd leading His flock.

*My sheep hear my voice,
and I know them, and they follow me;*

*And I give unto them eternal life:
and they shall never perish,
neither shall any man pluck them out of my hand.*

*My Father, which gave them me, is greater than all;
and no man is able
to pluck them out of my Father's hand.*

*I and my Father are one.
John 10:27-30*

I like to think of myself as a sheep
following the leading of the Lord.

I visualize a picture my grandson took
of the Bellingrath Gardens in Alabama.

The picture gives me a feeling of peace and rest
and brings to mind Psalm 23,

The Lord is my shepherd: I shall not want.
He maketh me to lie down in green pastures:

He leadeth me
beside the still waters.
He restoreth my soul:

He leadeth me
in the paths of righteousness
for his name's sake.
Psalm 23:1-3

I see my Shepherd leading me beside those still waters
totally restoring and refreshing my whole being.

I praise Him and thank Him
for continuing to lead.

I pray that my ears will always be open
to hear His voice, and
to follow Him.

Soliloquy # 500

Feelings of Inadequacy

There are times when I feel totally inadequate.
Then I need to remember God's Word:

Moses, that great man of God, felt inadequate.
(Exodus 3:11)

He asked God, *Who am I that I should....*
And God answered, *Certainly I will be with thee....*

As Moses passed his mantle to Joshua,
he encouraged him,

*Be strong and of good courage,
do not fear or be afraid....for the LORD your God,
He is the One Who goes with you.
Deuteronomy 31:6-8*

God also repeated His encouraging words to him.

*As I was with Moses, so I will be with you.
I will not leave you nor forsake you.
Joshua 1:5-6*

It is obvious that God was with his people
in the Old Testament,
but what about today?

According to Galatians 3:28, the apostle Paul,
who was the apostle to the Gentiles,
taught that there is now no difference
between the Jews and Gentiles.

He also exclaimed that nothing could separate us
from the love of God!

*I am persuaded that neither death nor life,
nor angels nor principalities, nor powers,
nor things present nor things to come,
nor height nor depth, nor any other created thing,
shall be able to separate us from the love of God
which is in Christ Jesus our Lord.
Romans 8:38-39 (NKJV)*

How then could it be possible to feel inadequate
considering these statements of God's love?

Yet, as if to put a final stamp on the subject,
I can claim my adequacy through Christ,

*I can do all things through Christ
who strengtheneth me.
Philippians 4:13*

Scriptures Used

Scripture:	Soliloquy Number:
Exodus 3:11	500
Deuteronomy 5:33	430
Deuteronomy 31:6, 8	444, 500
Joshua 1:5-6	500
Ruth 2:12	423
1 Samuel 16:7	426
2 Samuel 5:23-24	475
2 Kings 2:11	409
2 Kings 6:17	409
2 Kings 13:14	409
2 Kings 18:5-7	404
1 Chronicles 12:22-23	426
1 Chronicles 28:18	467
Nehemiah 9:5-6, 17	471
Job 1:21	460
Job 7:7	460
Psalm 18:28	415
Psalm 19:1	422
Psalm 19:14	425, 491
Psalm 19:1-2	475
Psalm 23:2	455
Psalm 23:1-3	499
Psalm 25:16-18	441

Psalm 34:5-11	446
Psalm 34:18	494
Psalm 36:5-7	472
Psalm 37:4-5	417
Psalm 37:23-24	419
Psalm 37:25	417
Psalm 45:6	433
Psalm 51:17	494
Psalm 63:6-8	450
Psalm 86:15	410
Psalm 89:1	410
Psalm 91:1,4	423
Psalm 92:1-2	455
Psalm 92:1-4	406, 412
Psalm 92:5, 12, 14-15	412
Psalm 92:1-2, 4-9, 12-15	431
Psalm 93:2	433
Psalm 96:11-12	474
Psalm 103:1-2, 11-18, 22	456
Psalm 116:15	443
Psalm 119:105	473
Psalm 139:14	466
Psalm 139:23-24	418
Psalm 139	442
Proverbs 2:1-8	
Proverbs 3:5-6	417, 476, 478
Proverbs 15:13	480
Proverbs 16:18	416
Proverbs 17:22	480
Proverbs 30:4-5	460
Isaiah 26:3	417
Isaiah 29:13	440
Isaiah 42:5	477
Isaiah 44:24	477
Isaiah 45:18, 21-23	429
Isaiah 55:8-9	469
Isaiah 55:11	433, 453

Jeremiah 6:16	428, 467
Jeremiah 9:24	419
Jeremiah 18:7-10	424
Daniel 5:20	424
Daniel 11:22	424
Amos 4:13	425
Amos 5:8	425
Micah 3:4	426
Micah 7:18	419
Zephaniah 2:3	484
Habakkuk 2:4	424
Habakkuk 3:17-19	411
Matthew 2:1-2	488
Matthew 2:11	488
Matthew 5:6	453
Matthew 6:33	476
Matthew 7:21-23	404
Matthew 10:29	468
Matthew 11:28	414
Matthew 11:28-29	467
Matthew 15:8	440
Matthew 15:21-28	458
Matthew 18:11	408
Matthew 21:8-9	402
Matthew 23:37	423
Matthew 24:7	484
Matthew 25:13	452
Mark 1:23, 27	447
Mark 10:14-15	407
Luke 2:52	438

Luke 15:2-10	408
Luke 19:40	474
Luke 21:26	424
John 1:11-12	458
John 3:16	437, 438
John 4;34	438
John 10:27-30	499
John 12:48-50	434
John 13:34-35	454, 495
John 15:33	439
John 16:33	441
John 17:7	473
Acts 1:11	452
Acts 5:29	433
Acts 17:1-3, 11-12	459
Acts 22:3	459
Romans 1:15	436
Romans 2:9-11	474
Romans 5:9	448
Romans 8:18	441
Romans 8:22	441
Romans 8:28	433, 435, 469, 478
Romans 8:34	490
Romans 8:38-39	485, 500
Romans 10:13	458
Romans 12:1-2	488
Romans 12:8	433
Romans 13:1	433
Romans 13:11-14	496
Romans 15:13	486
1 Corinthians 5:5	439
1 Corinthians 10:11	416
1 Corinthians 15:19	486
1 Corinthians 15:22	492
1 Corinthians 15:53, 57-58	497

2 Corinthians 1:3-4	469
2 Corinthians 5:7	430
2 Corinthians 5:14	454
2 Corinthians 5:21	437, 438
2 Corinthians 6:2	401
2 Corinthians 6:3-6	405
2 Corinthians 9:15	437
Galatians 3:26	465
Galatians 3:28	500
Galatians 5:16	430
Galatians 5:22-23	405
Ephesians 3:6-7	464
Ephesians 3:20	409
Ephesians 4:1-3	403
Ephesians 5:1	465
Ephesians 5:18	427
Ephesians 5:20	485
Philippians 1:9	433
Philippians 2:3	416
Philippians 2:10-11	429
Philippians 2:5-11	451
Philippians 3:13	486
Philippians 4:4-8	421
Philippians 4:8	427, 461, 491
Philippians 4:13	500
Philippians 4:13, 19	444, 447, 473, 478, 500
Colossians 1:9-11	462
Colossians 2:2-3	495
Colossians 4:5-6	496
1 Thessalonians 5:3	432
1 Thessalonians 5:9	448
1 Thessalonians 4:13-18	439
1 Thessalonians 4:14-17	482

1 Thessalonians 5:18	485
2 Thessalonians 3:16	480
1 Timothy 2:1-2	433
1Timothy 3:16	490
1 Timothy 4:4	420
1 Timothy 4:7-8	470
1 Timothy 4:12	402
2 Timothy 2:11-13	479
2 Timothy 3:1	484
Titus 1:2	448
Titus 3:1	436
Titus 3:7	448
Hebrews 4:12	418
Hebrews 4:16	490
Hebrews 5:12-13	457
Hebrews 6:10	483
Hebrews 9:27-28	432
Hebrews 11:32-40	469
Hebrews 12:1-2	413, 470
Hebrews 13:5	413
Hebrews 13:b	487
Hebrews 13:5-6	432, 444
James 1:17	416
James 4:6	416
James 4:10	494
James 4 14	487
1 Peter 1:13-15	448
1 Peter 2:2	457
1 Peter 5:2-4	436
1 Peter 5:7	447, 481
2 Peter 3:1-15	498

1 John 1:7	430
1 John 2:2	458
1 John 2:28	465
1 John 4:19	454
3 John 4	465
Revelation 2	454
Revelation 2:4	440
Revelation 5:12	409. 445
Revelation 11:15	438
Revelation 21:1	484
Revelation 21:3	441